The
Education *of*
the Presidents
of the United States

VOLUME 3: FRANKLIN D. ROOSEVELT TO GEORGE W. BUSH

2

Mother, Rebekah Baines ... she is one
the smartest, sweetest women
it has ever been my pleas...
know. That comment made my
beam over with pride. It
again served to impress up...
knowledge that my mother
not have an eq...

We were very b...
today ...

GEORG...

YALE

Capt. G.H.W. Bush '48

The
Education *of*
the Presidents
of the United States

VOLUME 3: FRANKLIN D. ROOSEVELT TO GEORGE W. BUSH

General Editor
Fred L. Israel
Department of History
City College of New York

Associate Editors
Michael Kelly
Department of History
The Gilman School

Hal Marcovitz
Staff Reporter
Morning Call (Allentown, PA)

Introduction by Arthur M. Schlesinger, jr.
Albert Schweitzer Chair in the Humanities
City University of New York

MASON CREST PUBLISHERS
PHILADELPHIA

Mason Crest Publishers
370 Reed Road
Broomall, PA 19008
www.masoncrest.com

Copyright © 2004 by Mason Crest Publishers. All rights reserved.
Printed and bound in the Hashemite Kingdom of Jordan.

1 3 5 7 9 8 6 4 2
First Printing

Library of Congress Cataloging-in-Publication Data

The education of the presidents of the United States / Fred L. Israel,
general editor ; introduction by Arthur M. Schlesinger, Jr.
    p. cm.
Includes bibliographical references (p.   ) and index.
  ISBN 1-59084-546-3 (Set) — ISBN 1-59084-547-1 (v. 1)—ISBN
1-59084-548-X (v. 2)—ISBN 1-59084-549-8 (v. 3)
  1. Presidents—United States—Biography.
  2. Presidents—Education—United States. [1. Presidents—Education.]
  I. Israel, Fred L.
  E176.1E34 2004
  973'.09'9—dc22
                            2003023310

Table of Contents

VOLUME 3: FRANKLIN D. ROOSEVELT TO GEORGE W. BUSH

Franklin D. Roosevelt
Chapter Thirty-one

F ranklin D. Roosevelt ranks as one of the most controversial presidents in American history. His administration (1933–1945) confronted two of the most important events of the twentieth century—the Great Depression and World War II. In handling these momentous problems, Roosevelt became a larger-than-life hero to millions—a president who could just do no wrong. Likewise, due to the fundamental changes in the nation's economy caused by his policies, millions of others came to hate "that man in the White House" because, they claimed, he undermined states' rights and individual liberty. Nevertheless, even his detractors agree that Franklin D. Roosevelt left an indelible mark on the United States.

Roosevelt died in office on April 12, 1945, less than three months after his inauguration for an unprecedented fourth term. He wrote no memoir, no autobiography, no account of his personal inner feelings and motivations. There is excellent documentation of the facts of Roosevelt's life, but despite collections of his personal letters, the reminiscences of family, friends, and others who were associated with Roosevelt in every conceivable way, and the many thoughtful studies that have been written about his life and presidency, the essence of Roosevelt the man remains elusive. Although because of illness he lost the use of his legs at age thirty-nine, Roosevelt never allowed himself to indulge in self-pity. He chose instead to face all the obstacles that confronted the people who had placed their trust in him. While others lacked the courage to depart from the old accepted rules of American politics, Roosevelt repeatedly took unprecedented risks. His dynamic leadership never ceased to convey a sense of trust, of assurance, and of bravery.

Franklin Delano Roosevelt was born at his family home, Springwood, in Hyde Park, New York, on January 30, 1882. Hyde Park is a small village overlooking the Hudson River about eighty miles north of New York City and five miles from the town of Poughkeepsie. By the time of Franklin's birth, several generations of Roosevelts had made their homes in the beautiful Hudson River valley. It is thought that the first Roosevelt in America came from Holland in the 1640s.

Franklin Roosevelt was born to a wealthy family—a family that had enjoyed immense privilege for many generations, a family that was far removed from the great world of the underprivileged. From the porch of their stately manor at Hyde Park, New York, was a magnificent view of the Hudson River valley and the Catskill Mountains beyond. Herds of cattle grazed the land, and rolling hills, fields of grain, greenhouses, grape arbors, flowering gardens, goats, dogs, and stables for riding horses and racing trotters filled the panorama.

Outwardly, Roosevelt's youth was a happy, privileged existence. It was a sequestered life in which his playmates were almost always countless cousins and the children from neighboring estates. Before he was fifteen, Franklin had accompanied his parents on eight European trips, each of several months duration. In Europe his parents socialized with the wealthy aristocracy. He was taken to the English manors of friends and relatives, to the French Riviera, and frequently to German spas. The summer when he was nine, his parents enrolled him for six weeks in a school in southern Germany in the hope of improving his German. The Europe he knew was that of the elite. With the exception of servants, rarely did young Franklin have contact with people who worked for their living.

Hyde Park had a fine family library. Before he had reached fourteen, Franklin had read Alfred Thayer Mahan's epoch-study *The Influence of Sea Power Upon History, 1660–1783* (1890) as well as books written by Mark Twain, Rudyard Kipling, and Francis Parkman. (At the Roosevelt Museum, one can read margin notes and comments made by young Franklin in many of these books.) One afternoon, his mother found him engrossed in reading *Webster's Unabridged Dictionary*. She asked "what on earth" he was doing. He replied that he was reading the dictionary because "there are lots of words I don't understand" and that he was "almost half way through."

In the autumn of 1896, Roosevelt's parents entered him at the Groton School in Massachusetts. Their aim was to prepare Franklin for college. This was the first time that Franklin would be attending a formal school, and the first time that he would be separated from his loving and doting parents. Mrs. Roosevelt recorded Franklin's departure in her diary: "We dusted his birds and he had a swim in the river....I looked on. And with heavy heart. It is had to leave our darling boy. James and I both feel this parting very much."

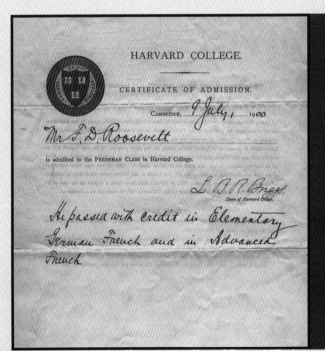

Harvard College in 1900 was, as it had been for some two hundred and fifty years, a school for the sons of America's most distinguished and wealthy families. Almost immediately, Franklin Roosevelt, now eighteen, plunged into a wide range of social, athletic, and extracurricular activities. He seemed released from the confines of Hyde Park and Groton. He tried out for nearly every athletic team but made only one intramural football team. Although he was now more than six feet tall, he weighed only one hundred and forty-five pounds, which was much too light for the varsity team. He was too slow for the track team and not strong enough to succeed at rowing. Though he joined the freshman glee club, in his sophomore year he lost out to better voices.

Franklin's wealthy father, James Roosevelt, had purchased Springwood and over the years had increased his land holdings to more than a thousand acres.

James Roosevelt's first wife died in 1876. Four years later, when James was fifty-two, he married Sara Delano, a sixth cousin who was half his age. Like her husband, Sara Delano came from an extremely prosperous merchant family. Sara had traveled to China as a girl, attended school abroad, and moved in the prominent social circles of London and Paris.

James Roosevelt had inherited a comfortable fortune and his greatest concern, especially after his second marriage, was his country squire's life among the Hudson River gentry. His financial investments yielded sufficient money to enable this type of luxury. Their marriage was serene until broken by James's death in 1900 at age seventy-two (Franklin was then eighteen).

Franklin had a secure and idyllic childhood. His half-brother was an adult when Franklin was born, so Franklin faced no rivals for the love and devotion of his parents. He grew up as an only child with the loving and doting attention of both parents and every privilege of an aristocratic boyhood. There were always servants at Springwood—a butler, cooks, maids, gardeners, and horse grooms. After Franklin's birth, James and Sara were able to continue their extensive travels and their life of affluence.

In later years, Sara Delano Roosevelt claimed that neither she nor her husband ever tried to influence young Franklin against his own tastes and inclinations. However, it is hard to imagine a mother more closely attached to a son or more preoccupied with monitoring his life and activities. His strong-willed mother expected that Franklin would, in due time, continue in the Delano and Roosevelt traditions of overseeing the family fortune. "I know that traditionally every mother believes her son will one day be president," Sara remarked in 1932, "but as much as I love tradition and believe in perpetuating good ones, that is one to which I never happened to subscribe."

Young Franklin rarely had contact with people who worked for their living. When he accompanied his parents on business trips in the United States, they traveled in a private railway car. Franklin's boyhood was the happy one of a young patrician—frequent trips abroad, summers swimming and sailing at the family vacation home on Campobello Island off the coast of Maine, and part of almost every year spent in New York City. However, Hyde Park remained Franklin Roosevelt's true home. Throughout his life—even when he was president—Roosevelt returned to this magnificent estate. Perhaps no president had a happier or more secure childhood than did Franklin Roosevelt.

James Roosevelt took an active interest in the Hyde Park public school but it probably never occurred to Sara to send Franklin there. She kept her son in an insulated world as long as she could. Young Franklin was educated by private tutors and governesses. His governesses were all European, and learning foreign languages made up a large part of Franklin's early education. He became fluent in French and could write German fairly well. (During World War II Roosevelt was able to converse with the French leader Charles de Gaulle, who refused to speak anything but French.) One governess assigned Franklin the task of writing essays in French

Groton was spartan compared to the comforts of Hyde Park. Franklin's six-by-ten-foot room was sparsely furnished. A curtain substituted for a door. The boys were awakened at 7 A.M.; breakfast was at 7:30; morning chapel at 8:15; and then off to classes. Dinner was served at noon followed by more classes and compulsory athletics. At supper, the boys wore blue suits, starched white collars and black patent-leather shoes. Evening chapel followed supper and then study hour. Endicott Peabody, headmaster of the Groton School, wrote, "He was a quiet, satisfactory boy, of more than ordinary intelligence, taking a good position in his Form, but not brilliant. Athletically, he was rather too slight for success. We all liked him."

A postcard shows the chapel at Groton as it appeared when Roosevelt attended the school.

Franklin D. Roosevelt, center, is photographed with the Groton School baseball team, October 1899. The curriculum at Groton stressed the classics. For example, in his first year, Franklin studied Latin, Greek, algebra, English literature and composition, ancient history, general science, and Bible studies. Franklin ranked in the top quarter of students throughout his four years at Groton. Never a great student, never overly popular with his fellow classmates, he did enjoy the distinction one year of being Groton's champion "high kicker" in football. He was not much of an athlete, and his principal contribution to the Groton School's sports program was to manage the school's baseball team.

on the social inequalities of the time. These essays, which have survived, may have been Franklin's first exposure to problems beyond the comfortable world of his loving family and their affluent friends. His teachers traveled with the family so that he could have his lessons anywhere in the world. Sara remained in total charge of her son's education and a governess either deferred to her wishes or left.

Franklin got along easily with the adults in his life. But when he was playing with children his own age, Sara noticed that he was inclined to be bossy and controlling. His earliest playmates were Edmund and Archibald Rogers, who lived on an estate near Springwood. At age six, Franklin began spending two hours each day at the Rogers' home learning reading, writing, and German from their governess. He soon was able to write short notes in German to his mother, which she lovingly preserved. Sara, determined for Franklin to improve his German, enrolled him in a public school in Germany for six weeks during one of the family's European trips. This was Franklin's only exposure to a public school, and his only exposure to the schedule of a schoolboy until he entered Groton five years later.

At age nine, encouraged by his mother, Franklin started a postage-stamp collection to which he continuously added, even when president. The extended Roosevelt/Delano families were involved in shipping and trading, especially with the Far East, so Franklin was always asking his relatives to send him mail and to bring him stamps. No country was omitted from his collection. When he went to Groton, and later Harvard, he took his stamp collection with him. During World War II, when as president he traveled to the Casablanca and Yalta conferences, his stamp collection accompanied him in a large wooden crate. Spending time with his collection provided a way for Roosevelt to relax. His formidable knowledge of world geography and of the most obscure potential battle sites—gained from philately—impressed his military aides. His collection became one of the world's largest, numbering scores of albums for practically every country.

Aside from formal subjects, Franklin was tutored in carpentry—making model boats, birdhouses, and toys. Like his distant cousin Theodore Roosevelt, Franklin developed a keen interest in ornithology (the branch of zoology concerned with the study of birds). He collected birds' eggs and nests, carefully recording his observations in a notebook. When he was eleven, he wrote a composition on "Birds of the Hudson River Valley" that so impressed his maternal grandfather that he gave Franklin a life membership in New York's American Museum of Natural History. Franklin even learned taxidermy, but soon left the messy job of stuffing his birds to the servants. Photography also fascinated young Franklin. Using an expensive tripod-mounted Kodak camera, he took dozens of family photographs, as well as self-portraits made using a timer. Many of these photos are on display at the Roosevelt Museum at Hyde Park.

Above all, Roosevelt's parents influenced his education by welcoming him into their adult world. They introduced him to their well-educated friends. With them, he attended cultural events, such as museums, the theater, and the opera in both Europe and the United States.

Throughout his life, Franklin Roosevelt loved reading. Springwood had an extensive library and Franklin was allowed to explore all of its offerings to his heart's content. He was a fast reader with a powerful memory, devouring books quickly and retaining startling amounts of information. As a teenager, Franklin especially liked books about the sea and naval history. (Sailing on his father's boat, the *Half Moon*, was a favorite hobby.) Before he had reached the age of fourteen, Franklin had completed

Franklin D. Roosevelt (right) playing the part of senile Uncle Bopaddy in W. S. Gilbert's *The Wedding March*, the Groton School senior class play, February 22, 1900.

Franklin Roosevelt majored in history and government, with English and public speaking as minors. He was not a great student, and did not take his studies seriously. As a result, his grades were usually a "gentleman's C." Extracurricular activities and social life were much more important to him. Charming, handsome, and extremely wealthy, Roosevelt took a cruise in the Caribbean with his mother and missed the first six weeks of Frederick Jackson Turner's famous course on the role of the frontier in American history. The few samples of his undergraduate writing that have survived are mediocre and uncritical.

1900-01.

HARVARD UNIVERSITY.

FACULTY OF ARTS AND SCIENCES.

The grade attained by *F. D. Roosevelt* ....in each of his studies for the year 1900–01 is given below.

GEORGE W. CRAM, *Recorder.*

	GRADE.			GRADE.			GRADE.			GRADE.	
	Course.	Half Course.		Course.	Half Course.		Course.	Half Course.		Course.	Half Course.
SEMITIC			GERMAN			ECONOMICS			ENGINEERING		
SEMITIC			GERMAN			ECONOMICS			MILITARY & NAVAL SCI.		
SANSKRIT			GERMAN			ECONOMICS			PHYSICS		
GREEK			FRENCH			ECONOMICS			PHYSICS		
GREEK			FRENCH 2a	C+		PHILOSOPHY			PHYSICS		
GREEK			FRENCH			PHILOSOPHY			CHEMISTRY		
GREEK			FRENCH			PHILOSOPHY			CHEMISTRY		
GREEK			FRENCH			PHILOSOPHY			CHEMISTRY		
LATIN	B		ITALIAN			PHILOSOPHY			CHEMISTRY		
LATIN		C+	ITALIAN			FINE ARTS			CHEMISTRY		
LATIN			SPANISH			FINE ARTS			BOTANY		
LATIN			SPANISH			ARCHITECTURE			BOTANY		
LATIN			ROMANCE PHIL.			MUSIC			ZOÖLOGY		
CLASSICAL PHIL.		C	COMP. LITERATURE			MUSIC			ZOÖLOGY		
ENGLISH 28		C	CELTIC			MATHEMATICS			GEOLOGY 4		C
ENGLISH			SLAVIC			MATHEMATICS			GEOLOGY 5		C
ENGLISH			HISTORY 1	C		MATHEMATICS			GEOLOGY		
ENGLISH			HISTORY			MATHEMATICS			MINERALOGY		
ENGLISH			HISTORY			ENGINEERING			MINING		
GERMAN			GOVERNMENT 1	C		ENGINEERING			ANTHROPOLOGY		
GERMAN			GOVERNMENT			ENGINEERING			HYGIENE		

The standing of every student in each of his courses is expressed, on the completion of the course, by one of five grades, designated respectively by the letters A, B, C, D, E. Grade E in any course denotes failure to fulfil the requirements of the course. "*Abs.*" indicates failure to obtain credit for the course, owing to absence from the final examination.

Alfred T. Mahan's *The Influence of Sea Power on History*. Years later, he fondly recalled the boyhood hours spent reading old naval logs and reports found in his maternal grandfather's attic. Undoubtedly, his mother's stirring stories of her seafaring ancestors and her own travels to Asia as a young woman greatly contributed to his interest.

Roosevelt's tutors generally informed Sara that he was a good student. However, Franklin was never subjected to competition or comparison with other students. He did not receive formal grades and report cards. While he had a vast memory, he displayed no tendency to think critically about the multitude of facts trapped in his mind. They seemed to be just another of his collections, neatly organized and easily retrieved at a moment's notice. His early school exercises show no attempt to connect these facts or to find any deeper meaning in them.

Sara and James Roosevelt began making plans for their son's teenage education early. When he was one year old, they placed his name on the future entrance list of the Groton School in Massachusetts. At that time, Groton was still the dream of Endicott Peabody, an autocratic yet inspiring Episcopal minister from a wealthy New England family. Peabody had been educated in England, and he dreamed of founding a school for American boys modeled after Eton and Harrow, the famous English boarding schools. Peabody planned to keep his school small and to maintain a family atmosphere with a strong emphasis on Christian ethics, athletics, and the virtues of public service. Friends of Sara and James Roosevelt had donated the land for Groton. Peabody and his educational ideas impressed the Roosevelts. Sara Roosevelt especially liked the idea that the school would be small. By the time Franklin entered Groton, however, it had become a prep school for rich boys and its graduates formed the top echelon of the social and business elite in the United States.

Franklin Roosevelt entered Groton in 1896. His Hyde Park friend Edmund Rogers entered the school with him, and his nephew "Taddy" Roosevelt (the grandson of James and his first wife), was a class ahead. Although the school offered a six-year program for boys between the ages of twelve and eighteen, Sara and James could not part with young Franklin, around whom their life centered, until he was fourteen. His enrollment at Groton marked the first time Roosevelt would attend a formal school in the United States, and the first time he would be separated from his loving parents. At Hyde Park, Franklin had been the center of attention; at Groton, he was one of one hundred and ten students, most of whom had already been at the school for two years.

The four years Franklin spent at Groton (1896–1900) made a lasting impact on him. He adapted himself readily to sharply different circumstances. Compared to the comforts of Springwood, Groton was spartan. His small room was sparsely furnished, and a curtain substituted for a door. Franklin had to conform to a rigid daily structure. Breakfast was at 7:30 A.M., morning chapel at 8:15, and then off to classes. Dinner was served at noon, followed by more classes and compulsory athletics. At supper, the boys wore blue suits, starched white collars, and black patent-leather shoes. Then followed evening chapel and study-hour, along with a nightly handshake from Reverend and Mrs. Peabody.

Much of what is known of Franklin's time at Groton comes from the chatty letters he sent to his parents. "I am getting along finely both mentally and physically," he wrote in his first letter home. The tone of his letters is persistently cheerful and optimistic, and at times a bit overdramatic.

There were nineteen students in Franklin's class, all boys from similar upper-class backgrounds. Compared to his classmates, Franklin was quiet and reserved. Nevertheless, he sang in the choir, played intramural football, criticized the food, and fully conformed to Groton's mores. The boys in his class had already formed friendships; Roosevelt was an outsider who had to work his way into the group. Some of his classmates, finding him priggish and superficial, called him the "feather duster." To make matters worse, he had a slight accent as a result of his European travels and his extensive study of foreign languages. He worked to lose his accent, which the other students considered an affectation. Although he was never overly popular with his classmates, one year Franklin did enjoy the distinction of being Groton's champion high-kicker, setting a school record.

The Groton years left Roosevelt with a belief that children of the upper classes had a duty to society—especially to the underprivileged. Undoubtedly this belief came from Endicott Peabody, who constantly worried about the poor and needy. Peabody's biographer describes him as something of a Christian Socialist concerned about the morals of the masses but almost oblivious to the economic and social problems caused by the industrial revolution. This remarkable man apparently stamped his values on almost every Grotonian. Roosevelt formed a lifelong friendship with Peabody. When Franklin married, Peabody performed the ceremony, and when Franklin took his first oath of office as president in 1933, Peabody recited the prayer.

"Very good," wrote Headmaster Peabody on the first monthly report to Franklin's parents. "He strikes me as an intelligent and faithful scholar and a good boy." The curriculum at Groton stressed the classics—in his first year, Franklin studied Latin, Greek, algebra, English literature and composition, ancient history, science, and the Bible. During his time at the school Franklin's grades averaged slightly less than B, and he ranked in the top quarter of students. In his final report, Peabody wrote, "He has been a thoroughly faithful scholar and a most satisfactory member of this school. I part with Franklin with reluctance." In an interview conducted during Roosevelt's 1932 presidential campaign, Peabody rephrased his observations: "[Franklin] was a quiet, satisfactory boy, of more than ordinary intelligence, taking a good position in his Form, but not brilliant. Athletically he was rather too slight for success. We all liked him."

Franklin D. Roosevelt entered Harvard University in 1900, when he was eighteen years old. Harvard was then, as it had been throughout its history, a school for the sons of America's most distinguished and wealthy families. Many of Roosevelt's Groton classmates entered Harvard with him. They lived in the same luxurious private suites of rooms, ate at the same Groton table rather than in one of the large common dining halls, and joined the same social clubs. Their world expanded only slightly to include graduates of other exclusive New England prep schools.

Franklin Roosevelt's main interest at Harvard became the undergraduate daily newspaper, the *Harvard Crimson*. In 1902, during his junior year, he was elected editor-in-chief. He wrote all the editorials, and for some years liked to describe himself as a former newspaperman, who through his editorials had fought for reform at Harvard. In reality, he had sought no reform more drastic than the laying of boards on the muddy paths between the Harvard buildings.

At Harvard, Roosevelt seemed released from the confines of Springwood and Groton, and he plunged into a wide range of extracurricular activities. He tried out for nearly every athletic team, but made only one intramural football team—although he had grown to six-foot-one, he weighed just one hundred and forty-five pounds, much too light for the varsity football squad. He was too slow for the track team, and not strong enough to succeed at rowing. Though Roosevelt joined the freshman glee club, in his sophomore year he lost out to students with better voices.

Thanks to Roosevelt's excellent preparation at Groton, he completed most of the course work for the B.A. degree in three years. Roosevelt's main interest during his senior year became Harvard's undergraduate daily newspaper, the *Harvard Crimson*. While a junior he was elected editor-in-chief of this four-to-eight page tabloid, and work on the newspaper occupied much of his senior year.

Roosevelt, who majored in American history and government with minors in English and public speaking, was not a great student. He did not take his studies very seriously, and as a result his grades were often a "gentleman's C." Harvard offered students a great deal of academic freedom and a top-quality faculty, but Roosevelt was unimpressed with his Harvard education. He later complained that it had offered him complicated theories but little in the way of practical and useful information. "I took economics courses in college for four years," he later remarked, "and everything I was taught was wrong."

When Roosevelt was a freshman, his father died. James Roosevelt bequeathed to his son an annual income of about $6,000. (In 1900 a male school teacher earned about $500 a year, so $6,000 was indeed a small fortune.) Franklin Roosevelt was charming and handsome, as well as wealthy; in addition, his distant cousin Theodore Roosevelt became president of the United States in 1901. Because of his name and family connections, Roosevelt attended a seemingly endless series of parties on the Boston-Cambridge circuit. That social activities, rather than scholarship, occupied most of his time at Harvard can be seen from a line written to his mother: "Am doing a little studying, a little riding and a few party calls."

Sara Roosevelt inherited Springwood and the rest of James's estate. (She had already inherited more than a million dollars when her father died two years earlier.) In his will, James Roosevelt had stipulated that he wanted Franklin "under the supervision of his mother." Sara immediately assumed this role, renting an apartment in Boston to be near her son—"near enough to the University," she noted in her diary, "to be on hand should he want me and far enough removed not to interfere in his college life."

The presence of Franklin's mother so close to Harvard gained him a reputation as a "mama's boy." And, while many a young lady drawn to this handsome young Harvard man was put off by his domineering mother's influence, Franklin learned how to tactfully handle her. Sometimes he gave parties in his mother's lavishly furnished apartment, but at other times he attempted to remain independent of her presence. However, he spent the summers following his freshman and junior years with her touring Europe, with time left for sailing at Campobello.

The most important event of Franklin's years at Harvard was his engagement to a fifth cousin, Anna Eleanor Roosevelt. Franklin had known Eleanor since she was a child, but their relationship did not blossom into romance until his senior year, 1903–04. Their engagement was announced in November 1904.

At first, Franklin had avoided telling his mother about his growing interest in Eleanor. When he finally announced his intention to marry his cousin, Sara Roosevelt was shocked. She was not pleased at the thought of another woman in her son's life, and tried to cool the relationship by urging the couple to wait before formally committing themselves. In an attempt to have Franklin forget Eleanor, she took him on a Caribbean cruise. And on hearing about a minor diplomatic post available in London, Sara attempted to use her connections to secure the position for Franklin so that he would have to leave the country. In the end, her efforts failed: their wedding took place in New York City on March 17, 1905. Franklin was twenty-three and Eleanor twenty-one. President Theodore Roosevelt, Eleanor's uncle, gave the bride away in a ceremony and reception that was the high point of the New York social scene that year. "Well, Franklin," the president said in his high-pitched voice, "There's nothing like keeping the name in the family."

Franklin and Eleanor delayed their honeymoon so that he could finish his first year at Columbia University Law School. He had failed two courses and had to

Franklin Roosevelt, age twenty-two, in formal portrait for Harvard University, April 1904. The most important event of Roosevelt's years at Harvard was his engagement to his fifth cousin, Anna Eleanor Roosevelt. Franklin had known Eleanor from the time they were children, but their relationship did not blossom into romance until his senior year in 1903. Their engagement was announced in November 1904 and their marriage took place in New York City on March 17, 1905. President Theodore Roosevelt, Eleanor's uncle, gave the bride away. The president was the main attraction at the wedding while the bride and groom were virtually ignored.

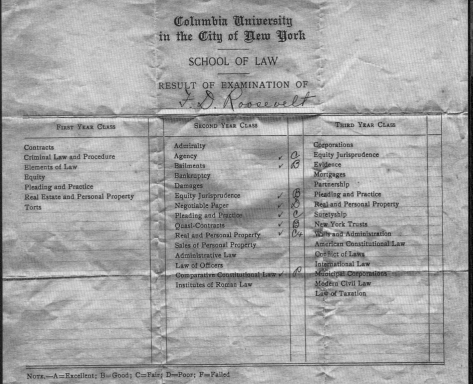

Columbia University
in the City of New York

SCHOOL OF LAW

RESULT OF EXAMINATION OF
F. D. Roosevelt

FIRST YEAR CLASS	SECOND YEAR CLASS			THIRD YEAR CLASS	
Contracts	Admiralty			Corporations	
Criminal Law and Procedure	Agency	✓	C	Equity Jurisprudence	
Elements of Law	Bailments	✓	B	Evidence	
Equity	Bankruptcy			Mortgages	
Pleading and Practice	Damages			Partnership	
Real Estate and Personal Property	Equity Jurisprudence	✓	B	Pleading and Practice	
Torts	Negotiable Paper	✓	D	Real and Personal Property	
	Pleading and Practice	✓	C	Suretyship	
	Quasi-Contracts	✓	B	New York Trusts	
	Real and Personal Property	✓	C4	Wills and Administration	
	Sales of Personal Property			American Constitutional Law	
	Administrative Law			Conflict of Laws	
	Law of Officers			International Law	
	Comparative Constitutional Law	✓	P	Municipal Corporations	
	Institutes of Roman Law			Modern Civil Law	
				Law of Taxation	

NOTE.—A=Excellent; B=Good; C=Fair; D=Poor; F=Failed

_____ Registrar

Franklin Roosevelt entered Columbia University Law School in the fall of 1904, squeezing class work into a full social calendar with less than happy results. Although the Columbia law faculty was one of the most distinguished in the nation, the professors elicited little response from Roosevelt. In the spring of his third year, he passed the New York State Bar examinations. He did not bother to finish his law school courses. Now twenty-five, he seemed perfectly suited to lead the life of a country squire just as his father had. Franklin and Eleanor had an annual income from trust funds of more than $12,000. (An average factory worker at that time earned about $300 per year.)

Twenty-two years later, in the autumn of 1929, Governor Franklin Roosevelt of New York was invited to address the Columbia Law School alumni dinner. Columbia's President Nicholas Murray Butler sat next to him. At some point during the evening, Butler was heard joking with the governor: "You will never be able to call yourself an intellectual until you come back to Columbia and pass your law exam." Roosevelt laughed and threw back his head. "That just shows how unimportant the law really is," he said.

pass make-up exams for these classes. Then, in June 1905, they took a grand European trip on which their family connection to President Roosevelt led to lavish treatment wherever they went. On their return to New York City, the young couple lived in a small house that had been rented and furnished by Franklin's mother.

Eleanor, however, was often unhappy. For most of her married life she had to live near Franklin's mother, who refused to fade into the background of the couple's life. "For the first year of my married life, my mother-in-law did everything for me," Eleanor later recalled. Franklin and Sara Roosevelt continued to have a warm relationship, and Sara remained a central figure in Franklin's life until her death in 1941. A depressed Eleanor repeatedly confided to her tear-stained diary her fear that Franklin had been attracted to her Uncle Theodore, not to her.

In the spring of 1907, Franklin Roosevelt passed the New York State bar examination and decided not to finish his degree at Columbia. Law school, he concluded, had no relationship to the actual practice of the law. Now twenty-five, he seemed perfectly suited to lead the life of a country squire, just as his father had done. The Roosevelts had an annual income from their trust funds of more than $12,000. (By contrast, a factory worker at that time earned about $300 per year.) Franklin and Eleanor Roosevelt's first child, Anna Eleanor, was born in 1906, followed by James in 1907, Franklin Jr. (who died shortly after his birth in 1909), Elliott in 1910, a second child named Franklin Jr. in 1914, and John in 1916. As Eleanor noted, for the first ten years of her marriage she was "just getting over having a baby or about to have one."

Roosevelt possessed an average legal mind. His looks, winning personality, and family connections soon brought him a law partnership, but the legal profession bored him. Politics, however, lit a fire in Roosevelt. His outgoing personality made him an obvious choice for public office. He served in the New York state legislature and as assistant secretary of the navy in Woodrow Wilson's administration before running for vice president on the Democratic ticket in 1920. After this losing race, his public career seemed to have come to an end when he was stricken with poliomyelitis and lost the use of his legs. But Roosevelt, with the assistance of his wife Eleanor, worked hard to return to politics. In 1928, he was elected governor of New York. Four years later, he was elected president of the United States, even though at the time his views on most national issues were unknown.

Franklin D. Roosevelt was given the best educational opportunities available to any American of his day. But academic subjects never really interested him. As a child he encountered no competition for the love, acceptance, and admiration of everyone that mattered to him. At Groton, and again at Harvard, he had to learn to compete and to succeed. Within his insulated experiences, he learned the skills that enabled him to face the broader world beyond. When he died in 1945, Roosevelt had made enemies who despised him and everything for which he stood, but he had also gained the love and respect of millions of people throughout the world.

—Fred L. Israel

Harry S. Truman
Chapter Thirty-two

Although today he is admired for his honesty, simplicity, and straightforward style, Harry Truman was not the most popular of presidents. He was thrust into the position in 1945 after the death of one of the most beloved presidents of all time, Franklin D. Roosevelt. After four terms in office, Roosevelt was the only president most young Americans had ever known. He proved a tough act to follow. Truman took over near the end of World War II, and was soon faced with the most critical decisions in the nation's history.

Truman was entirely different in background, education, and style from his predecessor. While Roosevelt had been born into wealth and privilege, Truman's life and upbringing were far more typical for Americans of the time. In the early years of the twentieth century, the United States was still a nation of farmers, though farmers and immigrants were moving into large cities in unprecedented numbers. Young Harry grew up on his grandparents' farm in Missouri and, as a young man, worked the farm alongside his father and brother. Truman lived most of his life in Independence, Missouri. It was small-town America, but closely connected to both urban and rural life. Kansas City, ten miles from Independence, was booming and growing into the largest city between St. Louis to the east and San Francisco to the west.

Of all the twentieth-century presidents, Harry Truman had the least amount of formal education. He was the only president elected in the century who did not attend college. Although this lack of education made Truman unusual for a modern day president, it made him quite typical at a time when the majority of Americans his age had not even finished high school. A late bloomer, he did not settle on a career in politics until he was thirty-eight years old. The years between completing his formal schooling and choosing his ultimate career served as a rather long apprenticeship. Numerous work, educational, and social experiences went into preparing him for his presidency.

Harry Truman was born in the small town of Lamar, Missouri, on May 8, 1884. He was the oldest of John and Martha "Mattie" Truman's three children.

Reading history was Truman's passion.

As a boy Harry read avidly. He claimed—doubtless with some exaggeration—to have completed every book in the Independence Public Library—even the encyclopedias—by the time he graduated from high school. Reading history was Truman's passion. On his twelfth birthday, his mother gave him an impressive four-volume set of books, bound in leather and trimmed in gold, entitled *Great Men and Famous Women: A Series of Pen and Pencil Sketches of the Lives of More than 200 of the Most Prominent Personages in History*. These books were anthologies of essays from Harper's and other leading American and English magazines. The authors included Edward Everett Hale, Thomas Macaulay, and young Theodore Roosevelt; the subjects ranged from Moses to President Grover Cleveland. By the time he was sixteen, Truman had read Jacob Abbott's twenty-two volumes of biographical studies of famous people of the ancient and medieval worlds. "Reading history, to me, was far more than a romantic adventure," wrote Truman. "It was solid instruction and wise teaching which I somehow felt that I wanted and needed."

A postcard shows Independence High School as it appeared at the turn of the century. Harry Truman graduated from Independence High School in 1901, when he was seventeen years old. He enjoyed all of his high-school subjects but did best in history.

When Harry was three years old, the family moved to the farm of Mattie's parents located not far from Kansas City. Truman's earliest memories were of farm work. It was here that his mother taught him how to read. When he had trouble making out the letters in the family Bible, Mattie took him to an eye doctor who fitted him with the thick glasses he wore for the rest of his life. The doctor and his parents warned Truman not to break them, so his opportunities to play rough games and sports were limited. Instead, young Truman spent a great deal of time reading.

The Trumans took an interest in their children's educations. In 1890, the family moved to the nearby town of Independence specifically because its schools were superior to those in the country. In Independence, John Truman operated a livestock business in addition to working a small farm. He was an ambitious man who failed in several business ventures in his efforts to get ahead. A hard-working perfectionist, he expected his children to do the best job possible, whether they were weeding the garden or studying for school. All the Truman children performed regular daily chores. Harry and his brother, Vivian, split the firewood, fed and watered animals, weeded the garden, mowed the lawn, and raked leaves in fall.

Truman's parents enrolled him in Sunday school at the Presbyterian Church. The Trumans were Baptists, but Mattie found the Presbyterian minister to be a most educated man. At church Truman first set eyes on Elizabeth "Bess" Wallace, who would one day become his wife. Class distinctions among white people were determined by religion in Independence, where much of the town's social life revolved around church functions. Presbyterians were the social elite; the Baptists ranked considerably lower. Through Sunday school and his own reading, Truman became familiar with the Bible and was able to quote numerous verses by heart—particularly the Sermon on the Mount: "Ye are the salt of the earth…Let your light so shine before men, that they may see your good works." He claimed he had read the Bible "three times through" by the time he was thirteen years old.

At age eight, Harry began first grade at the Noland School in Independence. He contracted diphtheria during second grade and missed most of the school year when complications developed. He was tutored during the summer to catch up to his classmates and did so well that he skipped third grade. At the Noland School, Harry received excellent grades in spelling, reading, deportment (conduct), arithmetic, language, and handwriting. (Although Harry was originally left-handed, his teachers made him learn to write with his right hand, a common practice at that time.) Years later, his first-grade teacher remembered him fondly, as would most of his teachers. He remembered them fondly as well. Truman took pride in having been a bit of a teacher's pet. He learned early in life that he could succeed by establishing a good rapport with people.

When the Trumans acquired a piano, Harry began to take lessons. At first, his mother, who had studied art and music at a women's college, taught him. He quickly moved on to lessons from his next-door neighbor, and when his ability to learn quickly outstripped her ability to teach, he began taking piano lessons twice a week in Kansas City. Harry showed talent. He loved music, especially the great classical works. He was apparently a favorite with his piano teacher as well. Mrs. Grace White opened a new world for him. Harry practiced at least two hours every day, often beginning at five o'clock in the morning. Mrs. White, a gifted teacher, took him to concerts in Kansas City when outstanding pianists performed. She took him to hear the Polish composer Ignacy Jan Paderewski play the piano at a Kansas City recital. Mrs. White introduced young Harry to him after the concert. At the time, Truman was trying to learn a work composed by Paderewski, his "Minuet in G." To his surprise, the composer sat down at the piano and demonstrated a stanza that was giving Truman trouble. (Years later, Truman entertained Winston Churchill and Josef Stalin with the same piece when they met at Potsdam near the end of World War II.)

Harry Truman took piano lessons in Kansas City for five years, even after he graduated from high school. He gave them up when he could no longer afford them. He recalled many times in later years that he had considered a career as a professional pianist. Although he moved on to other interests, Truman continued to enjoy classical music for the rest of his life.

When Truman was growing up, a high school education was not essential. Jobs were available to boys who finished sixth grade, and many went directly to work after finishing elementary school. Most boys who went on to high school were preparing for college and a professional career. Harry's parents were probably behind Truman's drive to continue his education through high school. Young Harry took on his first paying job during his freshman year. He worked before and after school at Clinton's drug store. After three months, his grades suffered. His father ordered him to quit and concentrate on his school work, making it clear that he thought school was more important.

High school lasted three years and included English, Latin, public speaking (known as rhetoric), logic, mathematics, science, and history. History was always Truman's favorite subject. An enthusiastic reader, he claimed to have read every book in the Independence Public Library by the time he was seventeen. His favorites were always history books, particularly biographies. For his twelfth birthday, his mother presented him with a four-volume set of books called *Great Men and Famous Women*. He was especially interested in military history and military leaders. His favorite book of the set was a volume called *Soldiers and Sailors*. The generals he most admired were Hannibal, Andrew Jackson, and Robert E. Lee. In Latin class, the students read Julius Caesar's account of his military campaigns. Truman and two friends were so inspired by a description of a bridge that Caesar's army built across the Rhine River that they spent days building a wooden model to match it. His favorite writers were Mark Twain and the poet Alfred Lord Tennyson. He continued to carry a copy of Tennyson's *Locksley Hall* in his wallet throughout his presidency. The one subject that always gave Truman trouble was spelling. His spelling difficulties would continue to plague him in his letters as an adult.

Truman also enjoyed Latin and algebra study sessions with his cousins, Nellie and Ethel Noland, and with Bess Wallace, who lived across the street from the Nolands. Cousin Ethel would remember, "I don't know whether they got much Latin read or not because there were a lot of fun going on." In Truman's senior year, he was on the staff of the school's first yearbook, which students voted to name *The Gleam* after Tennyson's romantic poem *Merlin and the Gleam*, which every tenth grader memorized. Truman graduated in 1901 at the age of seventeen. There were twenty-four girls (including Bess Wallace) and eight boys (including Charlie Ross, who later served in the White House as Truman's press secretary) in his graduating class. We do not know his high school grades because the school records were destroyed in a fire. He claimed to have been a good student, and we know that he and his teachers maintained contact for many years. In his memoirs, Truman repeatedly expressed admiration and gratitude to them, most of whom were unmarried women who devoted their lives to teaching. Truman felt he had learned human values from these women, values that surmounted book knowledge. From his teachers and parents, Truman

Harry Truman is in the back row, fourth from left, in this photograph of the Independence High School graduating class of 1901. Bess Wallace, his future wife, is on the far right of the second row. The class valedictorian, Charlie Ross, is seated at the far left of the front row; Ross and Truman would maintain a lifelong friendship.

learned the need for hard work and honesty. He learned to respect honesty, straightforwardness and simplicity, characteristics for which he is admired.

Around the time of Truman's high-school graduation, John Truman's business failed, leaving him with huge debts that affected the family for years to come. If college had been on Harry's horizon, it was no longer a possibility. He became interested in the U.S. Military Academy at West Point, partly because he was fascinated by military history, but mostly because it offered a free college education. His dreams of becoming a great general and attending the alma mater of his hero, Robert E. Lee, were not to be—but this was not for lack of trying. He and a friend, who was interested in an appointment to the Naval Academy at Annapolis, prepared together for the entrance examinations. They studied history and geography with their high school history teacher, Margaret Phelps. The panorama of history, as taught by Miss Phelps, began with Adam and Eve. Truman's efforts came to naught when he failed the eye exam and was told he was ineligible for the academy.

Rather than marching at West Point, Truman enrolled in a course at Spalding's Business College, a business school in Kansas City. He studied bookkeeping, stenography, and typing. Over the next few years, he worked at several entry-level jobs. Kansas City offered abundant choices for culture and leisure, and Truman enjoyed them, particularly concerts and the theater. He was working as a bank clerk when his family moved back to his grandparents' farm. Truman followed and spent the next eleven years as a farmer.

All the while, Truman was ambitious, but his ambitions were ill defined. He wanted to succeed and make something of himself, especially after he began courting Bess Wallace. He did not intend to spend his life as a farmer and tried several business ventures, all of which eventually failed. In his letters to Bess, he joked about a career in politics.

Politics fascinated John Truman, and he openly shared this interest with his oldest son. In 1900, Harry had worked as a page during the Democratic National Convention, which met in Kansas City. There he heard William Jennings Bryan, the populist Democratic presidential nominee who had broad support in farm areas. Bryan became his political hero. Despite his Democratic leaning, Truman also left work to hear Republican President Theodore Roosevelt speak in 1903.

While Harry was working on the farm, John Truman received a politically appointed job as road overseer in their portion of the county. The upkeep and repair of country roads was performed by local men with their horses. For the work, the men received a rebate on their school tax. Almost no one wanted the overseers job. When his father died in 1914, Harry took over this patronage position. Although it involved a great deal of work for little pay, it served Truman well later in his political career when he undertook the improvement of all the county's roads.

Truman led an active social life. He joined numerous organizations, including the Missouri National Guard. When the United States entered World War I in 1917, Harry volunteered for the army. He could have opted out of the war. At thirty-three, he was too old to be drafted. As a farmer, he was exempted from serving because farmers were considered essential at home. Also, his poor eyesight would have exempted him. However, he passed the eye exam and joined, helping first with recruiting efforts before he was sent to training camp. Both in the national guard and in the army, Truman served in the artillery, in which crews positioned and fired mounted cannons.

Military training and service served to further Truman's education. It helped him to see new possibilities within himself. He once said, "a leader is a man who has the ability to get other people to do what they don't want to do, and like it." During World War I, Truman discovered that he had this ability. Army companies elected their own junior officers, and to his surprise Truman found himself elected a first lieutenant. He had expected to serve as an enlisted man, not an officer. After some training in the United States, Truman was shipped off to France ahead of his company to attend artillery school. Most of the other officers at the school were college graduates and found the coursework considerably easier than did Truman. Once his company arrived, he was responsible for its training. He became the soldiers' instructor in surveying, engineering, trigonometry, and logarithms; mathematical calculations were necessary to make certain the large guns were aimed accurately. After the company's training ended, Truman was given command of a notoriously unruly group of men. He quickly established discipline and earned their loyalty and respect.

Between taking command in July 1918 and the Armistice in November 1918, Truman saw a considerable amount of action. He discovered that he could keep his cool while under fire and that other men would follow him. He was soon promoted to captain. The men he led and the loyalty he inspired in them served Truman well later when he had to campaign for votes. He had an extraordinary ability to remember people and until his death he exchanged letters with members of his World War I battery. Eventually his World War I friends became political supporters. Truman remained in the army reserves for many years and took part in training exercises every summer.

By the time the war ended, Truman was 35 years old and had still not really settled on what he wanted to do in life. He married Bess Wallace in 1919 (the Trumans would have one daughter, Mary Margaret). That same year Truman and an army buddy opened a men's clothing store. Because of a business recession, the business failed. Truman refused to declare bankruptcy, however, and spent the next fifteen years paying off his share of the debts.

Truman finally discovered his true calling when he ran for county judge in 1922. After taking office, he realized that he was an effective administrator and that he enjoyed the work. He made one more attempt at a formal education when he

Views of the main square of Independence, Missouri, circa 1909. When he was about thirteen years old, Truman began working at J. H. Clinton's drugstore in the center of town. He worked before and after school; it was his first paying job. "There must have been a thousand bottles to dust and yards and yards of patent-medicine cases and shelves to clean," Truman wrote years later to his daughter, Margaret. Truman recalled:

> I can remember the first $3.00 I received for working a week—seven days from seven o'clock until school time and from four o'clock until ten at night, all day Saturday and Sunday. I had to wipe off bottles, mop the floor every morning, make ice cream for sodas, and wait on customers. . . . That three silver dollars looked like three million and meant a lot more. I bought a present for Mamma and tried to give the rest of it to my dad and he wouldn't take it. It was as I say a great day all around when I got the $3.00.

enrolled in the Kansas City School of Law. It was the only law school in Kansas City, and it offered only night classes taught by local attorneys. In all, Truman took fourteen courses and received good grades. However, he did not continue after his second year, probably due to outside obligations and the pressure of supporting a family. The Kansas City School of Law awarded him an honorary degree in 1945.

Although Truman lacked the intellectual sophistication of an Ivy League education, his life experiences left him with common sense and an ability to work well with people. These qualities served him well when he led the U.S. at a challenging time in its history. During the first months of his presidency he made the decision to drop atomic bombs on Japan, which hastened the end of World War II. Truman also understood the challenges presented by the Cold War with the Soviet Union. He sent American troops to aid South Korea when it was attacked by North Korea in 1950. His 1948 decision to desegregate the armed forces preceded the civil rights movement of the 1950s and 1960s. Truman's middle-class, middle-American background helped him to understand the people he felt it was his duty to serve as president.

—Anne Marie Sullivan

Dwight Eisenhower
Chapter Thirty-three

When Dwight Eisenhower was fourteen years old he suffered what he believed was a minor scrape to his knee. That was hardly unusual. Dwight was a skinny but scrappy boy, quick with his fists but just as quick running away from tacklers on the football field or snaring grounders on the baseball diamond. Scraped knees and elbows, swollen lips, bloody noses, black eyes, and similar injuries were all common occurrences in the Eisenhower household. This time, however, the scraped knee proved to be a major problem when it became infected. The year was 1904, and penicillin would not be discovered for another twenty-four years.

The infection caused Dwight to fall into a delirium. A doctor was summoned to the Eisenhower home in Abilene, Kansas. For two weeks, the boy slipped in and out of a coma as the infection spread. Finally, with the infection creeping toward his abdomen, Dwight's physician feared that the boy's life was in danger. To save his life, the doctor decided that the infected leg had to be amputated.

During one of his rare periods of consciousness, Dwight heard his parents discussing the operation. Horrified, Dwight summoned his older brother Edgar to his bedside and made him promise not to let anybody cut off his leg. "Under no circumstances would they amputate my leg," Dwight recalled years later. "I'd rather be dead than crippled, and not be able to play ball." Edgar Eisenhower, who was two years older than Dwight, kept his promise. He slept on the floor of his brother's room, ready to scuffle with any surgeon who approached his brother intending to amputate.

After two more weeks, the infection subsided. Soon, Dwight's health returned, as did his quickness and competitiveness. On two good legs he would become a star athlete at Abilene High School and would later dazzle spectators as a halfback on the football team of the U.S. Military Academy in West Point, New York.

After his playing career was over, Dwight Eisenhower would call on the same determination that helped him endure a life-threatening infection to rise through the ranks of the U.S. Army and, as supreme commander of Allied forces in Europe, lead his troops to victory over Nazi Germany in World War II—an accomplishment that would pave the way to his election as the nation's thirty-fourth president.

Third Street looking East, Abilene, Kansas.

Dwight Eisenhower grew up with a liking for his hometown Abilene that he never lost. Third Street (pictured above in a photo taken about 1909) was Abilene's main street. On one side lived affluent families in stately Victorian homes, while on the other side were the simple wooden houses of working-class families such as the Eisenhowers.

Dwight Eisenhower was an average boy growing up in a small town in Kansas. He had ambition, but it was vague and unfocused.

Dwight is in the front row, second from left, in this 1901 photograph of his fifth-grade class at Lincoln Elementary School. Lincoln, one of two elementary schools in Abilene, lacked electricity and indoor plumbing. Younger students used slates for writing, paper being reserved for the fifth and sixth graders. About two-thirds of Eisenhower's class entered the town's high school.

David Dwight Eisenhower was born October 14, 1890, in Denison, Texas, a town just south of the Oklahoma border, where his parents had moved after his father's business failed. David and Ida Eisenhower had been married in 1885. As a wedding gift, David's father gave the couple one hundred and sixty acres of Kansas wheatland near Abilene, but David had no interest in farming and sold the acreage to buy a general store in the nearby town of Hope. Within two years, the business had collapsed.

By then, the Eisenhowers were the parents of a son, Arthur, and were soon to be parents of a second boy, Edgar. David Eisenhower found work cleaning locomotive engines in Denison. Soon, he summoned his family to join him. They lived in a small rented home—really not much more than a shack—in Denison, not far from the railroad roundhouse. Ida Eisenhower hated Denison and she hated Texas, but she toughed it out and refused to complain. It is likely that Dwight and his brothers inherited their silent determination and toughness of spirit from their mother.

David Dwight was the Eisenhower's third son. Ida Eisenhower named him David, after his father, but she never called him David, insisting that she did not want the boy to be confused with his father. She also abhorred nicknames, believing them undignified, and did not want her son called by the shortened name "Dave." Dwight, she was certain, could never be shortened into a nickname. Soon after his birth, Ida noted her son's name in the family Bible as "Dwight David."

(Much to her chagrin, her son Edgar would become known as "Big Ike" while Dwight was first "Little Ike" and eventually just "Ike," as people learned they could boil all those sounds in the Eisenhower name down to a single, friendly syllable.)

In Denison, the Eisenhowers lived just above the poverty line but Ida Eisenhower was a clever and resourceful woman who was able to feed and clothe her family despite her husband's paltry salary of $10 a week. Finally, David Eisenhower's brother-in-law, the foreman of a creamery in Abilene, offered David a job as a mechanic at the salary of $50 a month. David accepted, and the Eisenhowers returned to Abilene. The pay was not that much better than it was in Denison, but in Abilene the Eisenhowers would be back with family.

When the family returned to Abilene, eight-year-old Dwight was enrolled in Lincoln Elementary School, which was across the street from the family home at 201 South East Fourth Street. Dwight later described himself as a "lackluster" student; this is too modest an assessment, however, as he earned excellent grades throughout his school years. At Lincoln Elementary he enjoyed spelling bees and mathematics contests, regarding them as an outlet for his competitiveness. Later, in high school, Dwight would prove to be so gifted in geometry that he quickly solved every problem in his textbook, forcing his teacher to search elsewhere for problems that would challenge him.

"The introduction of plane geometry was an intellectual adventure, one that entranced me," Dwight Eisenhower later wrote. "After a few months, my teachers conducted an unusual experiment. The principal and my mathematics teacher called me to the office and told me that they were going to take away my textbook. Thereafter, I was to work out the geometric problems without the benefit of the book. In other words, the propositions, as well as the auxiliary problems, would be, for me, originals. This was a fascinating challenge and particularly delightful because it meant that no advance study was required. They said that for the remaining months, unless the experiment was terminated by them, I would automatically receive an A-plus grade."

His real love, though, was reading history. Mostly, he enjoyed books about great battles, particularly those that described the tactics and strategies of the ancient Greek and Roman generals. Later, he would extend his interest in military history to the American Revolution. This interest in military history should not be regarded as the initial sign that Eisenhower was destined for a future as a military leader. Dwight Eisenhower did not entertain the notion of soldiering as a career until he was twenty years old, and only then because a friend told him that the military academies did not charge tuition.

In addition, while he was fascinated by stories of warfare and quickly learned the dates and places of major battles, he was far less interested in the political reasons that prompted great armies to clash. "The battles of Marathon, Zama, Salamis, and Cannae became as familiar to me as the games (and battles) I enjoyed with my brothers and friends in the school yard," Eisenhower wrote years later. "I could never seem to get it into my head that all these things had happened two thousand years earlier—or that possibly I would be better advised to pay at least a little attention to current, rather than ancient affairs. Among all the figures of antiquity, Hannibal was my favorite."

David and Ida Eisenhower did all they could to discourage their son's interest in military science. The Eisenhowers were members of the River Brethren, a fundamentalist Protestant Christian church formed by former Mennonites from Pennsylvania; later, the Eisenhowers joined a congregation of Jehovah's Witnesses. As part of their religious beliefs, the Eisenhowers were pacifists. To cure her son of his interest in the art of war Ida Eisenhower locked his history books in a closet. She hid the key, but Dwight soon discovered its location and, whenever his mother was out of the house, he would unlock the closet and pore though his volumes of military history. "Whenever mother went to town to shop or was out working in her flower garden I would sneak out the books," he admitted in his memoirs.

Both David and Ida Eisenhower were dedicated readers; they filled their home with books, which were relatively rare among families living on the Great Plains. Each evening after dinner, David Eisenhower would gather his large family together and read the Bible. The boys were required to read passages from the Scriptures as well. The boys looked on the after-dinner Bible readings as a chore that had to be endured, and in their later lives none of the Eisenhower brothers would become devoted churchgoers.

The Eisenhowers had a large family. In addition to his older brothers Arthur and Edgar, Dwight had three younger brothers, Roy, Earl, and Milton. (A seventh son, Paul, was born into the Eisenhower family but died before his first birthday.) David Eisenhower was a stern, humorless man who demanded total obedience from his sons. He punished misdeeds severely, usually by a beating with his belt or a hickory switch. But David also believed in education—he had gone to college for a year himself before dropping out to marry and open the general store. One of his most severe beatings was administered to Edgar when David Eisenhower found out the boy was playing hooky from school to work at a part-time job. In later years, none of the boys—all of whom were beaten by their father at one time or another—would suggest that the thrashings were undeserved. "Had it not been for the application of leather, prolonged and unforgettable, my brother might have become an unhappy handyman in Kansas," Dwight explained. As it turned out, Edgar became a successful lawyer and a millionaire.

Dwight attended the seventh and eighth grades at Garfield School in Abilene, then in September 1904 enrolled as a freshman in what passed for Abilene High School—a few rooms on the first floor of city hall. The building also served as a jail and firehouse. (When a fire bell disrupted classes, male students were often drafted to help pull the fire engine through town.) At Abilene High, Dwight and his classmates learned English, history, mathematics, geography, and foreign languages. For the most part, Dwight was an A student.

It was during his freshman year at Abilene High that Dwight suffered the knee infection. The resulting illness forced him to drop out of school for the remainder of the year. When he returned to school in the fall of 1905 to repeat his

Abilene High School's baseball team, 1909. Dwight Eisenhower is in the front row, fourth from left.

Eisenhower had the good fortune to attend high school in a brand-new building with a newly hired faculty. "None of us could complain in our final high-school years about the competence or enthusiasm of our teachers," he recalled.

ABILENE CITY SCHOOLS
HIGH SCHOOL CREDIT SHEET

PUPIL'S NAME _Dwight Eisenhower_   FILING INITIAL _E_

STUDY	GRADE 1ST T	GRADE 2ND T	YEAR	TEXT	TEACHER	REMARKS
English 1	88	88	05-06			
Algebra 1	93⁷	93⁷	05-06			
Latin 1	93⁶	93⁶	05-06			
Physical Geog. 1						
Latin Comp	95⁴	95⁴	05-06			
Rhetoricals	86	86	05-06			
English 2	82+	82+	06-07	Johnson Lit	Daisy Martin	Lake Classics
Algebra 2	90-	90-	06	Wentworth	C. H. Brooks	½ yr. last half
Latin 2	85+	85+	06-07	Caesar	Lavonia Donica	Harper & Tolman
Ancient History 2	88+	88+	06-07	Myers	Pauline Sleeth	
Geometry 2	97+	97+	07	Phillips-Fisher	C. H. Brooks	First half
German 1	93⁷	93⁷	05-06			
English 3	I	II	07-08	Quackenbos	G. Dickinson	Classics
Geometry 3	I+	I+	07-08	Phillips-Fisher	M. Everette	
Latin 3	II	II	07-08	Cicero	L. Donica	
German 2						
Botany 1						
Eng. Hist	I+		07-08	Higginson & Channing	P. Williams	
Civics		II+	07-08			
English 4	II+	II+	'08-'09	Quackenbos	Lucy Dickinson	Johnson Simonds Classics
Latin 4						
German 3						
Physics 1	I	I+	08-09	C and C	C. H. Kesler	
American History 1	II+	II+	08-09			
Chemistry 1						
Econ	II+	I	08-09			

I hereby certify that the above is a true copy of the records in Abilene High School.

Date _____   _____ Principal

In 1904, Abilene High School consisted of five teachers and the principal, who also taught. The school was on the second floor of the city hall; the city jail and the town fire department were on the first floor. One room of the school served as a chapel, and teachers took turns conducting the daily devotional. In 1905, during Eisenhower's sophomore year, the school moved into a new building.

Several of the textbooks Eisenhower used as a student have survived. Interestingly, he scrawled in the margins his evaluation of his teachers: "good," "cross," one was scorned with "nothing." History, both ancient and modern, was Eisenhower's favorite subject. He idolized George Washington and he was fascinated by accounts of the Revolutionary battles of Trenton and Princeton, and by the encampment at Valley Forge.

Pictured above is Dwight Eisenhower's Abilene High School transcript.

freshman year, he started classes in a new red-brick building the community had erected to house the high school.

During the late 1860s, the dozen log huts that made up Abilene briefly became a boomtown at the junction of the Chisholm Trail and the Kansas-Pacific Railroad. Herds of Texas steers were driven to the stockyards there for transit to Chicago and the East. Education was not of primary interest to most residents. Some of the citizens of Abilene wondered why the town needed a high school in the first place. High school was still regarded as a luxury in the rural farm community; most boys dropped out of school following their elementary-school years to work in the fields or learn a trade. Jobs at the creamery were also plentiful. But all of the Eisenhower boys went to high school, even though if they had gotten jobs their wages would have helped out at home. When Dwight arrived for classes in the fall of 1905 there were thirty-four students enrolled at Abilene High School, twenty-five of them girls.

Somehow, the school managed to field baseball and football teams. Sports had long been Dwight's passion. The money he earned at odd jobs or by selling home-grown vegetables door-to-door was spent on sports equipment. As a high-school sophomore Dwight weighed one hundred and fifty pounds—small by football standards. He was a fierce competitor, though, and a leader on the team. In 1906, Dwight's first year on the football team, Abilene High School won all seven games it played by lopsided scores.

Dwight insisted on fair play and a strict adherence to the rules: no piling on after a tackle, no cheap shots at the other players. When Dwight caught one of his teammates violating the rules, his face would flush with anger and he would loudly and publicly dress down the other player. One time, when Abilene faced a team with an African-American player in the line, none of his teammates would play center—the position responsible for blocking the black student. Dwight, who never played center, volunteered for the assignment and spent the entire afternoon overmatched by the larger lineman. Nevertheless, at the end of the game Dwight shook hands with the fellow. "Rest of the team was a bit ashamed," he wrote later.

The Abilene team played much better than it looked. The team had just two footballs—one for practice, the other for games—and the school had no money for uniforms or equipment. The players provided their own uniforms: old sweaters as jerseys, saddle pads that were cut down and converted into shoulder pads, and stocking caps for helmets.

Dwight organized and became first president of the Abilene High School Athletic Association, which took on the responsibility of raising money for uniforms and sports equipment. The association also arranged travel to away games—usually, Dwight talked a friendly trainman into letting the team members ride in a freight car. The association was also responsible for finding opponents, which became something of a challenge due to Abilene's fierce reputation on the field. In Dwight's junior year, he could find only four opponents willing to face Abilene.

Dwight graduated from Abilene High School in May 1909. His brother Edgar was also a member of that graduating class, having dropped out of school for a time to work. The school yearbook, *The Helianthus*, identified Dwight as "Best Historian and Mathematician." Edgar was the real star of the class, though. The other students voted him most likely to be elected president of the United States.

The commencement speaker was Henry J. Allen, editor of the *Witchita Beacon* and a future Kansas governor and U.S. senator. Allen told the graduates, "I would sooner begin life over again with one arm cut off than attempt to struggle without a college education." His speech made a deep impression on Dwight.

Edgar and Dwight both wanted to go to college, but there was no money to pay the tuition. Edgar wanted to attend the University of Michigan, where he intended to study law. Michigan would have been fine with Dwight as well; in fact, any college with a football team would have suited him. Finally, the two boys came up with a plan. Dwight would work for a year, and his wages would help pay for Edgar's first year of school. In the second year, Edgar would drop out and take a job, which would help pay Dwight's college tuition for the first year. That fall, Edgar left for Michigan while Dwight found a job in the ice house at the creamery.

Dwight Eisenhower's year of labor stretched into two when his brother talked him into staying home for another year. During that time he earned a promotion to second engineer in the ice house, a position that required him to work from 6 P.M. to 6 A.M. He often had little work to do, which provided an opportunity to invite in friends from time to time for a few hands of poker—a game he loved and played meticulously, using his talent as a mathematician to constantly figure the odds. (Well into his White House years, the president steadfastly refused to draw to an inside straight.)

One of the friends who often came by the ice house was Everett Hazlett, son of an Abilene physician. Hazlett had received a congressional appointment to the U.S. Naval Academy in Annapolis, Maryland, but had flunked the entrance examination. While Eisenhower was working, Hazlett was spending a year studying to retake the test. It was Hazlett who first told Eisenhower that he could go to a military academy for free, an idea that intrigued Eisenhower. Hazlett urged him to write to Kansas's senators and ask for an appointment to Annapolis.

Eisenhower received a reply from Senator Joseph Bristow, who said that he awarded appointments to the academies to the boys who placed highest on a test. Eisenhower was one of eight candidates who showed up in Topeka on October 4, 1910, to take the test. He finished with the second-best score, hurt by surprisingly low marks on the history questions. Senator Bristow's examination had focused more on the reasons great battles were fought than on who had led the armies.

In any event, the senator could make two appointments. The young man with the highest score was given first choice; he selected Annapolis. Eisenhower was offered a place at the U.S. Military Academy at West Point. He was disappointed, as he had hoped to accompany his friend Hazlett to the Naval Academy.

June 9th
1911

En route to West Point, twenty-year-old Dwight Eisenhower stopped in Chicago to visit his high school friend Ruby Norman. She took this snapshot June 9, 1911, on South Michigan Avenue.

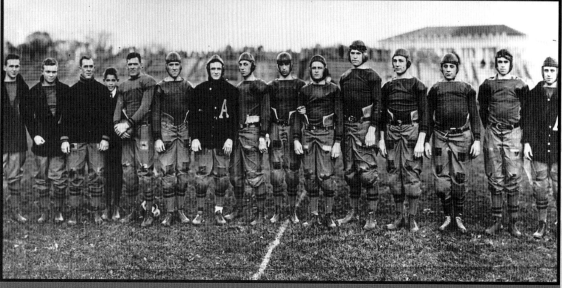

These two photographs show the West Point football team in 1912. In the top photo, Eisenhower is in the middle row, third from left. Omar Bradley, who also gained fame as a general during World War II, is in the back row, fourth from left. In the bottom picture, Eisenhower is second from left and Bradley is second from right.

Eisenhower considered appealing to Bristow, but in the end he accepted West Point. It was hard to pass up free tuition.

First, though, he had to pass West Point's entrance examination. Eisenhower had not been to school in two years, so he re-enrolled in Abilene High School to refresh his memory in chemistry, physics, and mathematics. He breezed through the Abilene courses, easily passed the West Point examination, and in June 1911 boarded a train for a long ride east.

Before leaving he did, of course, have to tell his pacifist parents that he was off to join the U.S. Army. "The only person truly disappointed was mother," he wrote. "She believed in the philosophy of turn the other cheek. She was the most honest and sincere pacifist I ever knew, yet at the same time she was courageous, sturdy, and self-reliant. It was difficult for her to consider approving the decision of one of her boys to embark upon military life."

Eisenhower arrived in West Point a twenty-year-old plebe, two or three years older than most of his classmates. On campus, he encountered a life most unlike that which he had known on the Kansas plains. Eisenhower had learned discipline and to obey his elders, but even the threat of a thrashing from his father did not compare to the intimidation he faced at the academy. Drill instructors, upperclassmen, and teachers were constantly barking orders at Eisenhower and the other plebes. Hazing was a way of life at West Point. Plebes were forced to stand in uncomfortable and exaggerated postures of attention, eat their meals with their feet raised off the floor, do countless push-ups, and perform ridiculous tasks, like collecting ants from an anthill. Eisenhower endured all with a steely resolve to succeed, but others were far less successful. His first roommate dropped out after a short time. (When Eisenhower became an upperclassman, he refused to haze the younger students.)

Eisenhower had been one of the best students at Abilene High School, but making good grades at West Point was much more difficult. During his four years at West Point his classroom performance was good but not great. He graduated sixty-first out of a class of one hundred and sixty-four.

West Point did have a football team, and Eisenhower made the squad on the first day of practice. By now, his skinny frame had filled out with muscle. Before the first game that fall, Army's star halfback, Geoffrey Keyes, sustained an injury. The coach played Eisenhower at halfback, and he responded by leading the team to two straight victories. His accomplishments on the gridiron were even written up in the *New York Times*.

Eisenhower's career in intercollegiate athletics would last only two seasons. In November 1912, shortly before the all-important game against Navy, he injured his knee during cavalry practice, tearing the cartilage and tendons. Eisenhower's football career was over, and the injury nearly ended his army career as well. Although the knee healed, army doctors refused to allow him to join the cavalry, which in those days was the most glamorous branch of the service. Instead, the doctors recommended Eisenhower for a career as an artillery officer, which would have required him to do little more than oversee large guns positioned at strategic defensive points on the coasts. Rather than accept that duty, Eisenhower decided to resign. He changed his mind when he was approved for infantry service.

He graduated from West Point in June 1915 and was commissioned as a second lieutenant. Eisenhower's rise through the ranks was steady and he would find himself serving under some of the army's greatest generals—John J. Pershing, Douglas MacArthur, and George C. Marshall among others. Eisenhower was promoted to brigadier general shortly before the Japanese attack on Pearl Harbor in December 1941, and was soon placed in command of Allied forces in the European theater of the war. He was in charge of the 1942 North Africa campaign, and as supreme Allied commander oversaw the D-Day invasion of France in June 1944. This invasion contributed greatly to the liberation of Europe and ultimate defeat of Nazi Germany. By the end of the Second World War, Eisenhower was perhaps the most popular U.S. hero.

Dwight Eisenhower, formal West Point cadet portrait, 1915.

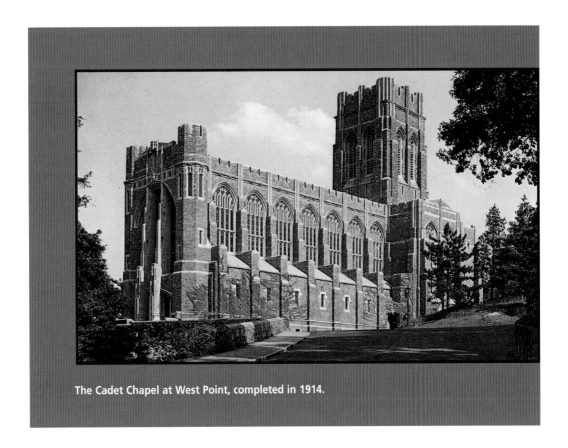

The Cadet Chapel at West Point, completed in 1914.

After the war, Eisenhower accepted the presidency of Columbia University in New York, then returned to the military to serve as commander of the multinational forces under the newly formed North Atlantic Treaty Organization. In 1952, the Republican Party convinced him to run for president. Eisenhower easily won election, and was reelected four years later. During his two terms as president, he forced the communist Chinese to accept terms ending the Korean War by threatening the use of nuclear weapons. At home, he launched the U.S. space program and sent troops to Little Rock, Arkansas, to enforce a federal court ruling that ordered the desegregation of schools. When his term ended in January 1961, Dwight Eisenhower and his wife Mamie retired to their farm in Gettysburg, Pennsylvania.

In March 1968, Eisenhower suffered his fourth heart attack in thirteen years. He would spend the last year of his life in Walter Reed Army Hospital in Washington, D.C. A few weeks before he died, Eisenhower was visited by General Vernon Walters, a long-time friend. Eisenhower told Walters that he did not expect to leave the hospital alive, but that he was satisfied with the way his life had turned out. "How can I complain when all the daydreams of my youth have been fulfilled?" he said. Dwight D. Eisenhower died on March 28, 1969.

—Hal Marcovitz

West Point, Class of 1915

The West Point Class of 1915 is referred to as "the class the stars fell on." Out of the one hundred and sixty-four graduates, fifty-nine became generals. Two—Dwight Eisenhower and Omar Bradley—rose to the five-star rank of general of the army; James van Fleet and Joseph McNarney attained four-star rank; seven became lieutenant generals (three stars); twenty-four were major generals (fifteen of these commanded divisions in combat); and twenty-four rose to brigadier or one-star generals. No other West Point class before or since has produced as many generals.

West Point graduates have made prominent contributions in non-military endeavors as well. From its beginning, graduates have been involved in non-military service—from selecting routes for railroads to exploring and mapping the nation's frontiers and designing public buildings. West Point graduates have become scientists, clergymen, mathematicians, engineers, businessmen, educators, diplomats, and statesmen, as well as soldiers.

John F. Kennedy
Chapter Thirty-four

Like so many public figures in his lifetime—Joseph P. Kennedy, Harry
Truman, Lyndon B. Johnson, to mention just a few—John F. Kennedy had a
profound regard for the importance of education in an individual's life and,
collectively, in the life of the nation.

Kennedy saw trained intelligence, particularly an understanding of history
and the analytical skepticism it encouraged, as essential ingredients of a democracy.
He greatly admired Thomas Jefferson, whom he saw as possibly the country's
smartest and most cerebral president. Kennedy once told a group of Nobel laureates
they were the greatest collection of brains ever assembled at the White House—
with the exception of when Thomas Jefferson dined there alone. Kennedy also
liked to quote Jefferson's observation that, "if a nation expects to be ignorant and
free, in a state of civilization, it expects what never was and never will be." In a
7,500-word message to Congress in 1963, Kennedy described education as "the
keystone in the arch of freedom and progress." He believed that federal monies
could improve the "quality of instruction" and reduce "alarming" drop-out rates.
Federal dollars were also needed to help colleges meet a projected 100 percent
increase in enrollments by 1970 and a 50 percent rise in students attending
secondary schools.

Kennedy saw ideas as a powerful influence on history and as essential to
successful leadership. "The men who create power make an indispensable
contribution to the nation's greatness," he said in a speech honoring the poet
Robert Frost at Amherst in October 1963, "but the men who question power make
a contribution just as indispensable, especially when that questioning is
disinterested, for they determine whether we use power or power uses us."

Kennedy himself was a published author. His first book, *Why England Slept*, a
revised version of his 1940 Harvard honors thesis, probed questions about how
England had allowed itself to become vulnerable to Nazi Germany by neglecting its
national defense. His second book, *Profiles in Courage*, published in 1956, celebrated
American politicians who risked their careers by opposing majority sentiment. The

Kennedy, John

RIVERDALE COUNTRY SCHOLE

Upper School Scholarship Report

Form_____   _____

SUBJ

Che

Civi

Dra

Engl

Fren

Gene

Geog

Germ

Gree

Hist

Latin

Man

Math

Mus

Penmanship

Physiology

Physics____

Kennedy, John

RIVERDALE COUNTRY SCHOOL

Upper School Scholarship Report

Form __I A__ for period ending __Feb 25__ 19_30_

SUBJECTS:

Subject		
Chemistry		
Civics		
Drawing		
English		C 3
French		D 3
General Science		
Geography		A 1
German		
Greek		
History		
Latin		
Manual Training		
Mathematics		B+2
Music		
Penmanship	B 2	
Physiology		
Physics		

Average   C+

Absence ____2____   Demerits _____

Creditable, Jack 75
Head Master.

Now for Honors

(over)

SYSTEM OF MARKING

Letters stand for achievement, and may be interpreted as follows:

A	high honors
B+	honors
B	good
C+	fair
C	minimum passing
D	failure
F	bad failure

Numbers represent the master's estimate of the boy's effort, and may be interpreted as follows:

1	exceptional effort
2	commendable effort
3	fair effort
4	indifferent effort
5	exceptionally poor effort

Reports are issued three times per term.

John Kennedy attended the Riverdale Country School in Riverdale, New York, from 1928 to 1930. On this report card, dated February 25, 1930, the encouraging headmaster noted, "Creditable, Jack. Now for Honors." According to the system of marking, Kennedy, nearing his thirteenth birthday, was a fair student who showed only moderate effort in his schoolwork.

book won a Pulitzer Prize and gave Kennedy standing as an uncommonly thoughtful senator worthy of consideration for the presidency.

Kennedy's regard for ideas grew out of at least three influences—his family setting, his childhood and adult struggles with health problems, and his exposure to teachers and fellow students at some of America's most distinguished educational institutions.

His mother and father were warm advocates of reading and exchange of ideas that introduced the young John Kennedy to the pleasure of books and the stimulation of debating ideas. Rose Kennedy encouraged a respect for book learning that registered forcefully on her nine children. Joe Kennedy's influence was even more decisive in encouraging his offspring to think for themselves. Family meals were occasions for discussions that kept his children abreast of current events and challenged them to argue against accepted truths. Sending his two eldest sons, Joseph Jr. and John, to study in England with Harold Laski is a case in point. When Joe Jr. graduated from Choate in 1933, his father decided that some exposure to Laski, a prominent socialist academic at the London School of Economics, would be a valuable experience. Rose considered this "a little wild and even dangerous," but Joe, convinced it would encourage greater independence and sharpen his son's ability to argue the case for a more conservative outlook, ignored his wife's concern. And when Joe Jr. returned after a summer trip to Russia with Laski and described the advantages of socialism over capitalism, Joe told Rose, "If I were [Joe and Jack's] age[s] I would probably believe what they believe, but I am of a different background and must voice my beliefs." Joe Sr. made it clear that he cared much less about their different outlooks than that they had reached independent judgments.

Jack's medical ills also made him more thoughtful and respectful of ideas. Considerable amounts of time in bed recovering from childhood maladies and subsequent chronic intestinal and back problems helped him develop lifelong reading habits that served him during his political career. More important, a variety of possibly life-threatening and painful ailments—spastic colitis, Addison's disease, the malfunctioning of his adrenal glands, unrelenting back difficulties, and chronic prostate infections (prostatitis)—moved Kennedy to be more reflective than he might otherwise have been about human nature and the human condition. It made him fatalistic but also intensified his determination to live life to the fullest. As a result of this, he refused to be intimidated by accepted wisdom and was open to unconventional ideas.

Kennedy's formal education reinforced and intensified his attraction to the proposition that a trained mind ensured a richer, more productive life. This was not evident at the start of his schooling. After attending the local Edward Devotion public school in Brookline, Massachusetts, for two years, when Jack was seven he and nine-year-old Joe Jr. were sent to a local private school, Dexter. There, unlike at Devotion, which had shorter hours, they could be supervised from 8:15 A.M. until

4:45 P.M. This schedule freed Rose Kennedy to give more attention to her daughter Rosemary, who was mentally retarded and required home tutoring. Rose also saw Dexter as a guard against the mischief—the "state of quixotic disgrace," she called it—for which Joe Jr. and Jack had an affinity. To their father, Dexter, an elite institution, would bring his sons together with their Beacon Hill counterparts, the offspring of social register families like the Storrows, Saltonstalls, and Bundys.

In September 1927, after the Kennedy family moved to Riverdale, New York, Jack began attending the private Riverdale Country Day School, where he excelled in his studies in the fourth and fifth grades. In the sixth grade, however, when Joe Jr. went to the Choate boarding school in Wallingford, Connecticut, Jack's work suffered, falling to a "creditable" 75, a report of February 1930 stated. Despite his undistinguished school record—or possibly because of it—Joe and Rose decided to send Jack to private boarding school as well. But instead of Choate, Rose enrolled Jack in the Canterbury School in New Milford, Connecticut. This was an exclusive Catholic academy run by a priest and staffed by fourteen teachers for ninety-two students. Of the twenty-one students in the school's 1930 graduating class who continued on to college, seven went to Yale, seven went to Princeton, and one went to Harvard.

Although attending a boarding school marked Jack Kennedy as a privileged child, he did not appreciate being sent so far away from home. He was homesick and struggled to make a creditable record. English, math, and history were fine, but he felt a little overwhelmed by science and Latin; poor grades in these subjects drove his average down to 77. "In fact, his average should be well in the 80s," the headmaster recorded. In a letter to his mother, Jack admitted he was "doing a little worrying about my studies, because what [the headmaster] said about me starting of[f] great and then going down sunk in."

In the fall of 1930, when he was thirteen, Jack was more interested in current events and sports than any of his studies. Football, basketball, hockey, squash, skating, and sledding were his first priorities, but feeling closed off in the cloistered world of a Catholic academy made him increasingly eager to keep up with the state of the world. He wrote to his father from Canterbury, "Please send me the Litary [sic] Digest, because I did not know about the Market Slump until a long time after, or a paper. Please send me some golf balls." A missionary's talk one morning at mass about India impressed Jack as "one of the most interesting talks that I ever heard." It was all an early manifestation of what his later associate Theodore C. Sorensen described as "a desire to enjoy the world and a desire to improve it; and these two desires, particularly in the years preceding 1953, had sometimes been in conflict." In 1930, however, pleasure seeking clearly stood first.

After a year at Canterbury School, Jack was not keen to return, but wished instead to follow Joe Jr. to Choate. Joe Sr. acquiesced to his son's request, and in September 1931 Jack joined his older brother at the storied New England academy. Choate was not quite on a par with the older, more elite, prep schools of Andover,

CANTERBURY SCHOOL

NEW MILFORD, CONNECTICUT

Record of John Kennedy, Form II

From November 1 to December 6, 1930.

Any average from 90% to 100% is accounted "Very Good"; from 80% to 90% "Good"; from 70% to 80% "Fair"; from 60% to 70% "Poor"; and below 60% "Unsatisfactory".

SUBJECT	DAILY WORK	EFFORT AND APPLICATION	FORM AVERAGE
English II	86	Good	71.69
Latin II	55	Poor	64.35
History II	77	Good	67.00
Mathematics II	95	Good	61.69
Science II	72	Good	66.62
Religion II	75	Fair	78.46
AVERAGE: 77.00			

This report is not quite so good as the last one. The damage was done chiefly by "Poor" effort in Latin, in which Jack got a mark of 55. He can do better than this. In fact, his average should be well in the 80's.

N.H.

Rose and Joseph Kennedy decided to send their son Jack to a boarding school. He was enrolled in the Canterbury School in New Milford, Connecticut, an exclusive Catholic academy run by a Catholic priest and staffed by fourteen Catholic teachers for ninety-two students. Of the twenty-one students in the school's 1930 graduating class going to college, seven went to Yale, seven to Princeton, and one to Harvard.

His fair academic work at Canterbury corresponded with an undiagnosed illness that restricted Kennedy's activities. Between October and December 1930, he lost nearly six pounds. In May 1931, Kennedy left school with appendicitis and did not return. He completed his year's work with the help of a tutor at home.

Exeter, St. Mark's, or St. Paul's, but it was distinctive enough—part of a wave of boys' boarding schools that had been founded in the 1880s and 1890s.

Within sharp bounds, Jack rebelled against school and, indirectly, parental authority at Choate. His schoolwork continued to be uneven—strong in English and history, subjects in which he had substantial interest, and mediocre at best in languages, which required the sort of routine discipline that he found difficult to maintain. His low grades in Latin and French compelled him to attend summer session in 1932, at the end of his freshman year. Rose later remarked on how concerned they were about Jack's health during his Choate years. But "what concerned us as much or more, was his lack of diligence in his studies; or, let us say,

Kennedy's classmates and teachers remembered him as a charming, irreverent young man with a sense of humor and a passion for sports and the good life.

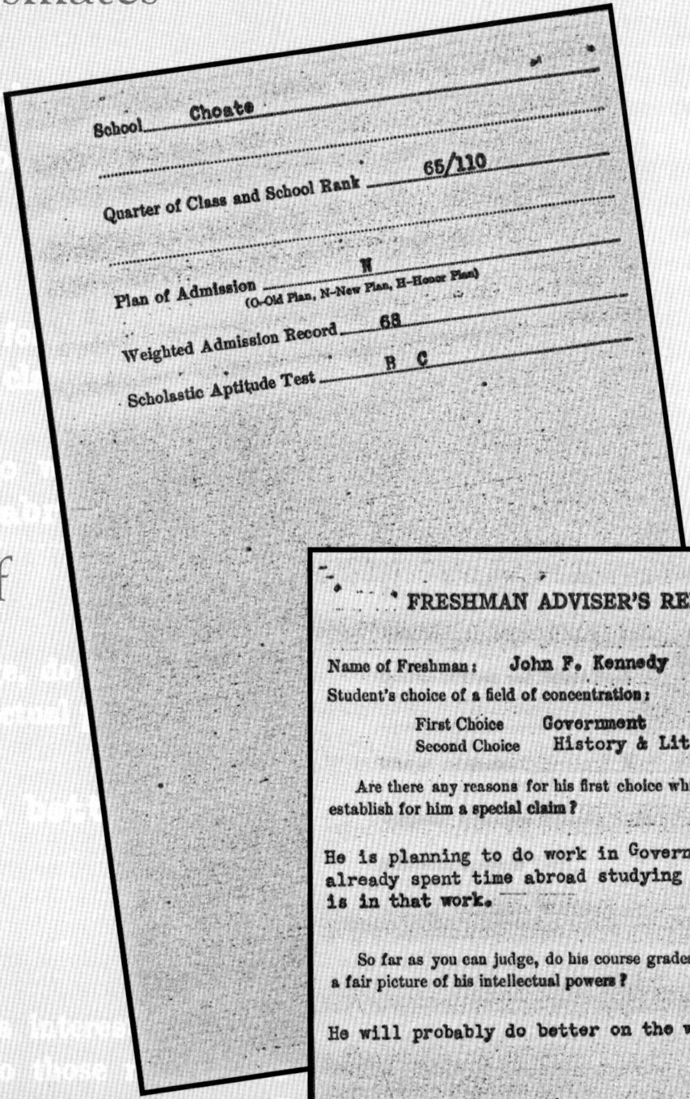

School _____ Choate _____

Quarter of Class and School Rank _____ 65/110 _____

Plan of Admission _____ N _____
(O–Old Plan, N–New Plan, H–Honor Plan)
Weighted Admission Record _____ 68 _____
Scholastic Aptitude Test _____ B C _____

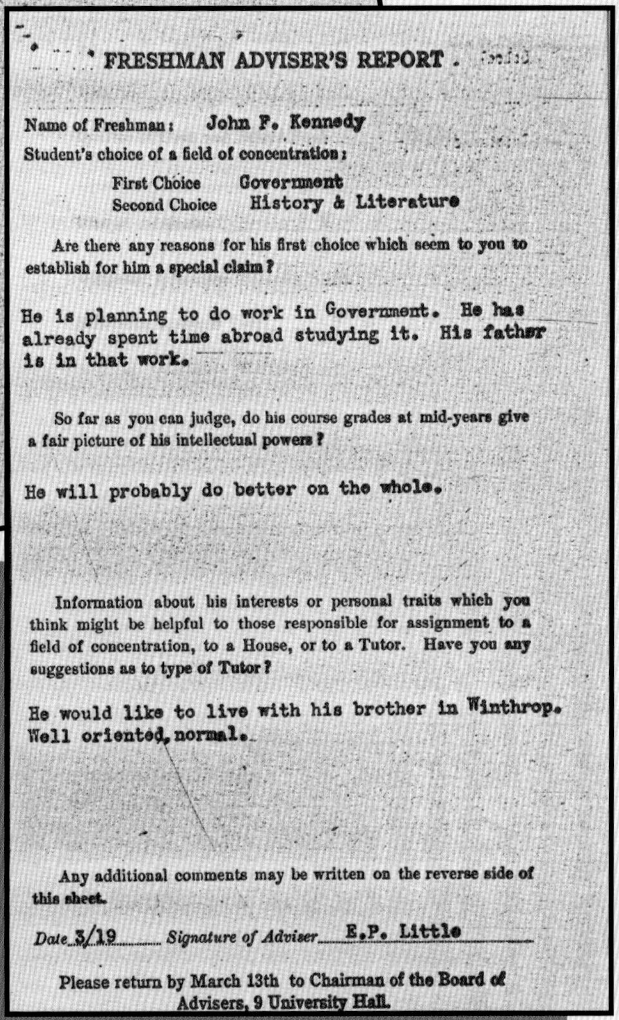

FRESHMAN ADVISER'S REPORT

Name of Freshman: John F. Kennedy
Student's choice of a field of concentration:
    First Choice   Government
    Second Choice   History & Literature

    Are there any reasons for his first choice which seem to you to establish for him a special claim?

He is planning to do work in Government. He has already spent time abroad studying it. His father is in that work.

    So far as you can judge, do his course grades at mid-years give a fair picture of his intellectual powers?

He will probably do better on the whole.

    Information about his interests or personal traits which you think might be helpful to those responsible for assignment to a field of concentration, to a House, or to a Tutor. Have you any suggestions as to type of Tutor?

He would like to live with his brother in Winthrop. Well oriented, normal.

    Any additional comments may be written on the reverse side of this sheet.

Date 3/19   Signature of Adviser   E.P. Little

Please return by March 13th to Chairman of the Board of Advisers, 9 University Hall.

John Kennedy attended Harvard College from 1936 to 1940. During his first two years, his academic record was unimpressive. Pictured above is his freshman "adviser's report," dated March 19, 1937.

    Kennedy's classmates and teachers remembered him as a charming, irreverent young man with a sense of humor and a passion for sports and the good life. While the university policy stressed the importance of merit, social snobbery still dominated undergraduate life.

TUTORIAL RECORD—19 37 - 38

John F. Kennedy — Winthrop — Govt
Class / Name / House / Concentration / Plan / Special Field

Correlation Field

READING AND ESSAYS / COMMENTS

Ford - Dictatorship in the modern World
Hoover - Germany Enters Third Reich
Mussolini - Autobiography
Seldes - Sawdust Caesar
Finer - Mussolini's Italy
Marx - Communist Manifesto
Lenin - State and Revolution
Armstrong - We or They
Beard - Economic Basis of Politics
Lindsay - Essentials of Democracy
Essay on These three books
Arnold - Folklore of Capitalism

Kennedy was ill during part
of the year, and did no very
large quota of tutorial work.
Though his mind is still
undisciplined, and will probably
never be very original, he
has ability, I think, and gives
promise of development.
Plan A recommended

Date / Tutor

lack of 'fight' in trying to do well in those subjects that didn't happen to interest
him....Choate had a highly 'structured' set of rules, traditions, and expectations
into which a boy was supposed to fit; and if he didn't, there was little or no
'permissiveness.' Joe Jr. had no trouble at all operating within this system; it suited
his temperament. But Jack couldn't or wouldn't conform. He did pretty much what
he wanted, rather than what the school wanted of him."

During his years at Choate, Jack remained more interested in contemporary
affairs than his classes. But although he "conspicuously failed to open his
schoolbooks," Choate's headmaster recalled, he "was the best informed boy of his
year." One classmate remembers that Jack was able to answer between 50 and 60
percent of the questions on the popular radio quiz show *Information Please*, while
the classmate could only get about 10 percent of them right. Jack's academic work
was good enough in his junior and senior years to allow him to graduate in the

middle of his class and gain admission to Princeton, which he attended briefly before transferring to Harvard in the fall of 1936.

During his first two years at Harvard, Jack largely continued the pattern he had established at Choate. His academic record was unimpressive: a B-minus in Government the first year and a B in English the second were offset by grades of C and C-plus in French, History, and a second Government course, his major interest.

Jack's Harvard classmates and teachers remember a charming, irreverent young man with a fine sense of humor and a passion for sports and the good life. He certainly showed no overt interest in the campus activism provoked by the Depression, FDR's New Deal, and the challenges to democracy and capitalism from fascism, Nazism, and communism. There is no indication that he read any of the

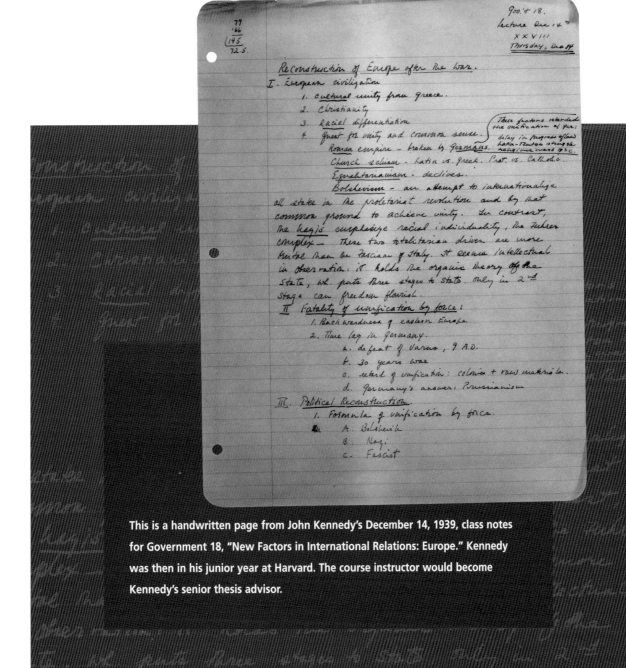

This is a handwritten page from John Kennedy's December 14, 1939, class notes for Government 18, "New Factors in International Relations: Europe." Kennedy was then in his junior year at Harvard. The course instructor would become Kennedy's senior thesis advisor.

popular progressive journals of the day—the *Nation*, *New Republic*, or *New Masses*—or gave much, if any, heed to the parades and protest demonstrations organized by students eager to have a say in public affairs. He had little use for doctrinaire advocates who "espoused their causes with a certitude which he could never quite understand."

His focus remained on the extracurricular and social activities he found more enjoyable, and stamped him out as one of the many students at Harvard more interested in earning the social standing attendance and graduation provided than the book learning needed to advance a career. Although James Bryant Conant, who became Harvard's president in 1933, stressed the importance of "meritocracy"—a university focused more on the intellect and character of its students than their social origins—social snobbery continued to dominate the undergraduate life of the university. Jack's first two years on campus were a reflection of these mores. Football, swimming, golf, and service on the Smoker and Annual Show committees occupied his freshman year, while junior varsity football and swimming, the Spee and Yacht clubs, and service on the business board of the *Harvard Crimson* filled his second year.

During these two years, however, Jack gave indications that he had more than a passing interest in public issues. His academic work began to demonstrate a substantial engagement with political leadership and how influential men changed the world. He read several books on recent international and political history, and more revealing, he wrote papers on King Francis I of France and Enlightenment philosopher Jean-Jacques Rousseau. His essays focused on the uses of political and intellectual power to alter human relations.

Nothing may have contributed to Jack's affinity for politics more than his repeated trips to Europe between 1937 and 1939, especially after his father became ambassador to Britain in 1938. The excursions became as much an opportunity for Jack to school himself about European power politics as about the traditional historical sites tourists visited in Western and Eastern Europe. The trips sparked Jack's interest in writing about the origins of Britain's appeasement policy and the coming of World War II. Jack's compelling central argument was one originally made by Alexis de Tocqueville over a hundred years before: popular rule does not readily lend itself to the making of effective foreign policy. Democracies, Jack asserted, have a more difficult time than dictatorships in mobilizing resources for their defense. Only when a pervasive fear of losing national survival took hold could a democracy like Britain or the United States persuade its citizens to "give up their personal interests, for the greater purpose."

Jack's thesis and later book marked the beginning of his entrance into politics. Some biographers have seen Jack's decision to run for Congress in 1946 as the result of his older brother's death in World War II and Joe Sr.'s pressure on Jack to replace his brother, who intended to run for high office. But Jack's interest in politics was more the product of his Harvard education and travels than of his

John Kennedy graduated from Harvard College in June 1940, *cum laude*, with a major in history and government. These pages are his Harvard transcript.

JOHN FITZGERALD KENNEDY   S.B. cum Laude June 20, 1940   Field of Concentration Government

Name of course	Description	Instructor
1936-37:		
English 1	History and Development of English Literature in Outline	Professor Munn
Economics A	Principles of Economics	Professor Burbank
History 1	European History from the Fall of the Roman Empire to the Present Time	Professor Merriman
French F	Introduction to France	Professor Morize
1937-38:		
English F1	Public Speaking	Asst. Professor Packard
Fine Arts 1e	Interpretation of Selected Works of Art: an Introduction to Art History	Professor Koehler
Government 1	Modern Government	Professors Holcombe and Elliott
History 32a1	Continental Europe: 1815-1871	Professor Langer
History 32b2	Continental Europe: 1871-1914	Professor Langer
Government 302	New Factors in International Relations: Asia	Asst. Professor Hopper
1938-39 Fall Term:		
Economics 61a1	The Corporation and its Regulation	Professor Mason
English A-11	English Composition	Messrs. Davis, Gordan, Bailey and McCreary
Government 7a1	The National Government of the United States: Politics	Professor Holcombe
Government 9a1	State Government in the United States	Professor Hanford
Government 181	New Factors in International Relations: Europe	Associate Professor Hopper
History 551	History of Russia	Asst. Professor Karpovich
1939-40:		
Economics 11b2	Economics of Socialism	Dr. P. M. Sweezy
Economics 62b2	Industrial Organization and Control	Professor Mason
Government 3a1	Principles of Politics	Professor Elliott
Government 4	Elements of International Law	Associate Professor P. S. Wild
Government 22	Theses for Honors	Members of the Department
Government 8a1	Comparative Politics: Bureaucracy, Constitutional Government and Dictatorship	Professor Friedrich
Government 10a2	Government of the British Commonwealth of Nations	Professor Elliott
Government 281	Modern Imperialism	Associate Professor Emerson

1 Indicates 1st half year course; 2 Indicates 2nd half year course.

John Kennedy spent the summer of 1939 traveling in Europe, ostensibly researching his senior thesis. His father, Joseph P. Kennedy, was Franklin D. Roosevelt's ambassador to Great Britain, so young Kennedy had access to an array of prominent people. Kennedy thought that the outbreak of war on September 1, 1939, would delay his Harvard senior year. In this September 13, 1939, letter to the college registrar, Kennedy, now twenty-two, explained that his father had sent him to Glasgow to assist the more than two hundred American citizens rescued by a British destroyer after a British liner carrying 1,400 passengers from Liverpool to New York had been sunk by a German submarine. The embassy staff had been so rushed because of the war that no regular member could be spared. This was Kennedy's first experience in hands-on diplomacy.

Kennedy, J.F.

THE FOREIGN SERVICE
OF THE
UNITED STATES OF AMERICA

AMERICAN EMBASSY

1, Grosvenor Square,
London, W.1.

September 13, 1939.

Oct 2

Bureau of Registration,
Harvard University,
Cambridge, Mass.

Dear Sirs:

As I am now working in charge of the Committee for the evacuation of the "Athenia" survivors, and due to the lack of transportation, it appears now that I shall not be able to return back to America before the 29th of September.

As this may get me back several days after the official entry, I found it necessary to advise you.

I hope that this will not endanger my standing, and I shall endeavor to get back as quickly as I can.

Very sincerely yours,

John F. Kennedy

John F. Kennedy, 40.

brother's demise and his father's insistence on a public career. Part of the message Jack took away from Choate and Harvard was that much was expected of those to whom much had been given. Jack saw his entrance into politics as a case of public service privileged Americans educated at private boarding schools and Harvard were trained to give.

Jack's regard for quality education registered forcefully on his presidency. During his thousand days in the White House, he repeatedly argued the case for expanded federal aid to education. He believed it essential if the United States were going to compete effectively in the Cold War. He saw a better educated population as not only raising the country's standard of living but also as a way to make America more attractive to Third World countries being wooed by communists promising a better life.

Although tensions over segregation, complaints that federal aid would undermine traditional ideas about separation of church and state, and budget constraints defeated Kennedy's legislative requests, he would surely have passed education bills in a second term when, like Lyndon Johnson, he would have had large congressional majorities. No comprehensive assessment of John F. Kennedy's life and political career can neglect his schooling and subsequent views on education.

—Robert Dallek

A photograph of the 1936 Harvard freshman swimming team. John Kennedy is in the back row, third from left.

Lyndon B. Johnson
Chapter Thirty-five

Rebekah and Sam Johnson spent months trying to talk their boy into going to college, but young Lyndon always refused. He hated studying, and disliked the restrictions on his time and behavior that had been placed on him in high school. Still, Rebekah and Sam persisted. Rebekah Baines Johnson was a woman of culture and refinement. She was a college graduate herself—rare for a woman in Texas's backwater Hill Country. She directed the plays at the local high school and gave elocution lessons in the parlor of the Johnson home. When Lyndon graduated from high school, she urged him to attend the nearby Southwest Texas State Teachers College.

Sam Johnson's efforts to get his son into college were more halfhearted. Sam was a farmer and high school dropout who lacked the refinement and education of his wife. He certainly knew the value of a college degree, however—he had served in the Texas legislature, working side-by-side with men who had gone to college. When it came to giving fatherly advice about what direction to take in life, Sam Johnson would often relay some ill-advised homespun wisdom to his boy, which Lyndon often found difficult to accept. "My daddy always told me that if I brushed up against the grindstone of life, I'd come away with far more polish than I could ever get at Harvard or Yale," Lyndon Johnson said years later. "I wanted to believe him, but somehow I never could."

By early 1927, Lyndon was eighteen years old and working on a road construction crew in rural south-central Texas. The back-breaking labor paid just two or three dollars a day, but at night Lyndon was free to go to dances and saloons and run with his friends, who were constantly on the lookout for ways to have fun and get into mischief.

One night in February 1927, Lyndon Johnson went to a dance in the town of Fredericksburg, not far from the Johnson home. Things had not been going well for him on the road crew. Lyndon had gotten into an argument with his boss and was probably going to lose his job. That night in Fredericksburg he wore a white silk shirt and swaggered around the dance hall, looking for trouble. It didn't take long

Johnson's biographer Robert Dallek noted that, "At school, Lyndon was constantly in trouble. His early academic work was good. However, he began to have behavior problems in the higher elementary grades. He wouldn't do his homework, and even rebelled against going to school. One observer in the Johnson home remembers that Rebekah [LBJ's mother] 'had a hard time getting him up in the morning and getting him to school.' A record of his school attendance from 1920 [when Johnson was in the eighth grade] shows that out of 180 school days he was absent 50 times and was tardy on 30 of the 130 days he was present." Pictured below is Johnson's third-grade report card.

"Never trouble another for what you can do for yourself"

PUPILS

PROMOTION--Satisfactory averages on all subjects; or a general average standing of 70 with no yearly average on any one study below 50 will be required for promotion. To be promoted this card must be presented upon your entrance in school next year.

"There is nothing so kingly as kindness and nothing so royal as truth."

Certificate of Promotion.

THIS CERTIFIES THAT Lyndon Johnson has attained the required standard in conduct and in the branches of study for promotion and is hereby promoted from Third Grade or year of course to Fourth Grade or year of course

Given this .... day of ....

Carrie Yett Teacher

Superintendent

"The best part of knowledge is that which teaches us where knowledge leaves off and ignorance begins."

Published By C. A. Bryant Co., Dallas, Texas.

"He that ruleth his own spirit is greater than he that taketh a city"

TEXAS
TEACHERS' MONTHLY REPORT
TO PARENTS

Johnson City Public Schools

PUPIL Lyndon Johnson

Age 7 grade or year of course 3

School .... District No. 11

Year 1915 1916

Carrie Yett, Teacher.

TO PARENTS

The school can do but little without the hearty co-operation of the home. We therefore send you a report each month to keep you informed as to the conduct, standing and progress, that you may better assist us in accomplishing satisfactory results. To this end we request you to examine this report carefully each month to give due credit and praise for all good marks, and remove, if necessary, the principal cause of all poor ones--irregularity in attendance and improper conduct.

Should there be any delay in the presentation of this report or any neglect in its preparation, or anything of any unsatisfactory character, you will confer a favor by calling attention to it immediately. Frequent visits by parents encourage teachers and pupils.

L C Fawcett Superintendent.

'Never put off till tomorrow what you can do today"

Published By C. A. Bryant Co., Dallas, Texas

Report for year beginning .... day of .... 191.... and Ending .... day of .... 191....

Reading, Spelling, Writing, Drawing, Arithmetic, Grammar, Geography, Physiology, Agriculture, Texas History, U.S. History, Civics, Composition, Physical Geography, Literature, General History, Algebra, Geometry, Physics, Application, Deportment, Days Absent, Times Tardy

Sept., Oct., Nov., Dec., Jan., Feb., Mch., Apr., May, June, Yearly Avg., Page Reached

Scale of grading: A+ = 95-100, A = 90-95, B+ = 85-90, B = 80-85, C+ = 75-80, C = 70-75, D+ = 65-70, D = 60-65

TO THE TEACHER

This report contains full information regarding the attendance, deportment and progress of the pupil. Fill the blanks regularly and carefully at the close of each month and send them to parents promptly. See that they are returned with proper signatures. Make all entries with pen and ink. Exercise such care that it will not be necessary to erase. The manner in which your reports are made will be a good index to the general character of your school. If rightly used, this report will prove to be a valuable medium of communication between you and the parents. Have frequent written tests on work passed over by all pupils. Require thorough work. Let your test be fair and sufficient. Honest patrons will sustain the honest teacher. Frequently bring or send work of your pupils to this office for inspection by other schools.

SCALE OF GRADING

E-excellent; 90-100. V-very good; 80-90. G-good; 70-80. F-fair; 60-70. P-poor; 50-60. Marks below F on studies and below 90 on conduct are considered unsatisfactory.

The parent or guardian will please sign below and return promptly to teacher.

Sept.
Oct. Rebekah B. Johnson
Nov. Rebekah B. Johnson
Dec. Rebekah B. Johnson
Jan.
Feb.
March
April
May

"The best thought of the community must be in close sympathy with the schools."

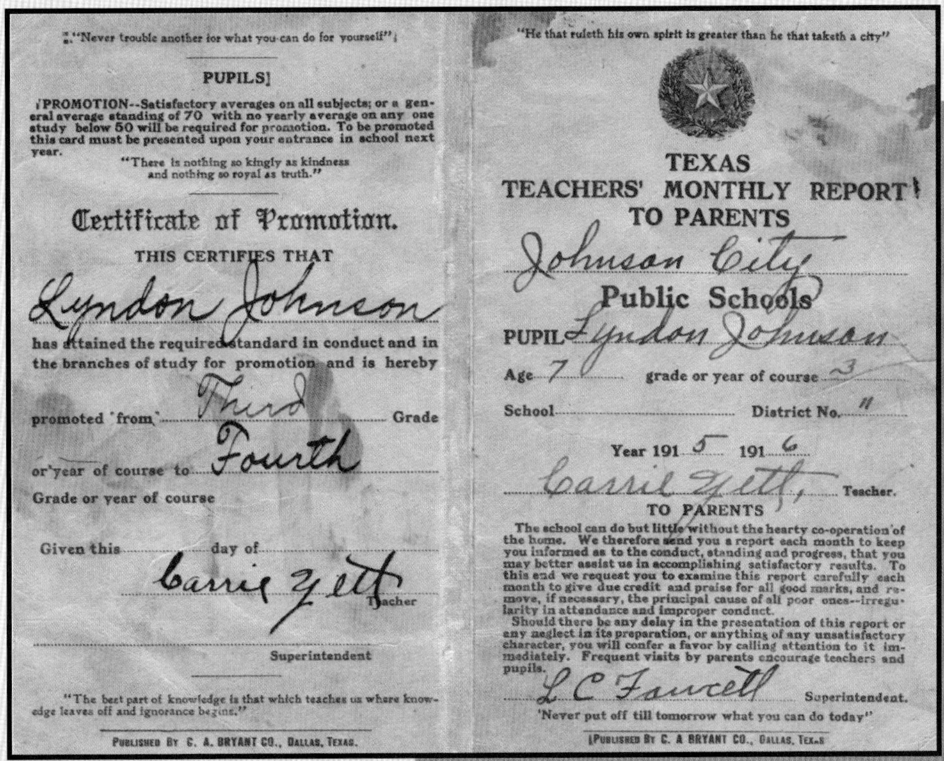

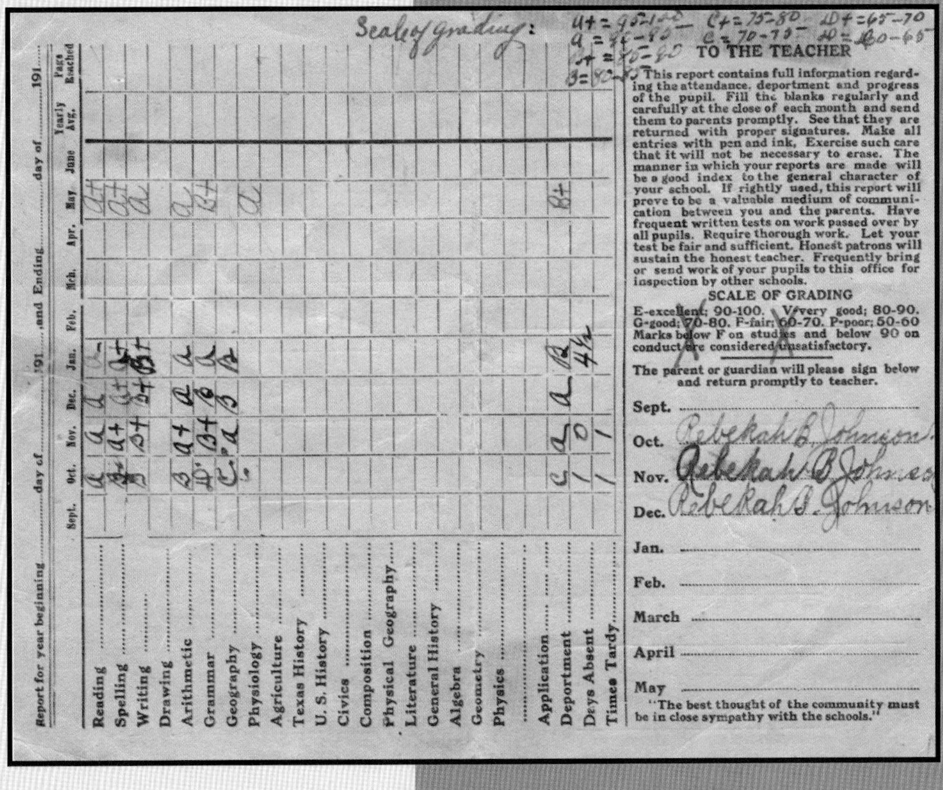

54   *Elson Grammar School Reader Book One*

VOCABULARY:
tåsk—work; business; toil; labor.
gål'-lant—brave; noble; high-spirited.
fāith'-ful—trustworthy; honest; sincere.

WORDS AND PHRASES:
"lone post of death"   "sail and shroud"
"wreathing fires"   "splendor wild"

SOMEBODY'S MOTHER*
(AUTHOR UNKNOWN)

1

THE woman was old, and ragged, and gray,
And bent with the chill of the winter's day.
The street was wet with the recent snow,
And the woman's feet were aged and slow.

2

She stood at the crossing and waited long
Alone, uncared for, amid the throng
Of human beings who passed her by,
Nor heeded the glance of her anxious eye.

3

Down the street with laughter and shout,
Glad in the freedom of "school let out,"
Came the boys like a flock of sheep,
Hailing the snow piled white and deep.

4

Past the woman so old and gray,
Hastened the children on their way,

*From Harper's Weekly. Copyright, 1878, by Harper & Brothers.

Somebody's Mother   55

Nor offered a helping hand to her,
So meek, so timid, afraid to stir,
Lest the carriage wheels or the horses' feet
Should crowd her down in the slippery street.

5

At last came one of the merry troop,
The gayest laddie of all the group;
He paused beside her and whispered low,
"I'll help you across if you wish to go."

6

Her aged hand on his strong young arm
She placed, and so, without hurt or harm,
He guided her trembling feet along,
Proud that his own were firm and strong.

7

Then back again to his friends he went,
His young heart happy and well content.
"She's somebody's mother, boys, you know,
For all she's aged and poor and slow;

8

"And I hope some fellow will lend a hand
To help my mother, you understand,
If ever she's poor, and old, and gray,
When her own dear boy is far away."

9

And "somebody's mother" bowed low her head,
In her home that night, and the prayer she said,
Was, "God be kind to the noble boy,
Who is somebody's son and pride and joy."

ELSON
GRAMMAR SCHOOL READER
BOOK ONE

FIFTH GRADE

MEMORANDUM

THE WHITE HOUSE
WASHINGTON

June 7, 1968

MR. PRESIDENT:

Last week on a ride around the Ranch, you told us about a
poem which influenced you as a boy -- the story of a boy
who shows compassion for an old woman. You mentioned
that it may have appeared in the 5th grade edition of
Elson's Readers.

Your memory was 100% accurate. The Library of Congress
couldn't find the book, but the Office of Education did.

Here is the poem.

Ervin Duggan

Attachment

In the last months of his presidency, Lyndon Johnson became increasingly
reflective about what had shaped his thinking process that led to the social
programs called the "Great Society." Ervin Duggan described one such incident.
Ervin Duggan, assistant to the president, to President Lyndon B. Johnson,
June 7, 1968. Elson, *Grammar School Reader* (1911), book one, fifth grade, pp. 54–55.

for him to find it. Lyndon provoked a fight with a hulking farm boy, who responded by unleashing a torrent of fists that the tall and lanky Lyndon Johnson could not fend off. With his fancy white shirt covered in blood, Lyndon limped home, his nose and spirit broken. "It made him realize he wasn't 'cock of the walk,'" recalled his cousin, Ava Johnson Cox.

The next morning, while Rebekah Johnson nursed her boy's wounds, Lyndon told her he was ready to go to college. He said, "All right, I'm sick of working just with my hands and I'm ready to try and make it with my brain."

Johnson City is located in Blanco County, Texas, about twenty-five miles west of the state capital of Austin. It was founded in 1879 by James Polk Johnson, a nephew of Lyndon's grandfather, Sam Johnson Sr. The Johnsons were a prominent family in Hill Country by the time Lyndon Baines Johnson was born on August 27, 1908, but they were by no means wealthy citizens. Few people in Hill Country were well off in those days. People in Blanco County were poor and mostly illiterate. Their land produced few crops. Indoor plumbing was a rarity in Blanco County homes. Electricity was nonexistent.

The thirty-sixth president of the United States was born on his father's farm near the town of Stonewall, on the north bank of the Pedernales River, the oldest of five children. Rebekah Johnson sent her boy to the local one-room Junction School when he was four years old, a year before most children were expected to begin school. Clearly, he was not ready for the experience. He was bright enough—by that age Lyndon was already reading—but he was shy and unwilling to participate in class. When the teacher, Kate Deadrich, told Rebekah that Lyndon refused to read aloud in class, she told her to let Lyndon read while sitting on her lap. It worked. Still, Lyndon didn't last too long in Miss Kate's class. After three months, he contracted whooping cough and had to stay at home for the rest of the school year.

Rebekah Johnson had never enjoyed the pioneer life on the farm near Stonewall. In September 1913, she convinced Sam to buy a home in Johnson City, about ten miles from the farm. Sam bought one of the finest homes in Johnson City, but it was hardly luxurious. Johnson City, with a population of about three hundred, had no paved roads, no gas lines to provide heat and light, and just a few telephones and automobiles. The downtown consisted of a saloon, diner, barbershop, drugstore, three churches, and a courthouse. There was also an elementary school, where Lyndon was enrolled shortly after his family moved to Johnson City.

Now a bit older and out of his shell, Lyndon Johnson was a rambunctious and ill-behaved boy who craved attention and exasperated his parents. Every night when Sam would get home from the farm, he would ask, "Well, what has Lyndon done today?" When Rebekah or his younger sisters would tell on him, Lyndon could often count on receiving a thorough spanking from his father. At school, he would underachieve well into his high school years. He refused to do his homework or study for tests and was often truant from school. In 1920, Johnson City school records showed that of one hundred and eighty days of school, Lyndon Johnson was absent fifty times and tardy thirty times.

Luzia Casparis, one of his elementary school teachers, described him as a "little hellion." Once, when Lyndon had gone several days without turning in his homework, Casparis told him he would have to remain inside for recess to make up the work. When the bell rang for recess, Lyndon defiantly walked out of the school, spitting at his teacher as he walked by. To punish the boy, Casparis locked him in a storage room. Lyndon pounded on the door and screamed so loudly that when she finally relented and let him out, he burst through the doorway so hard that he fell and bloodied his nose.

At the end of the 1922 school year, Lyndon was so far behind in his school work that he was told he would have to go to summer school or be held back. To make up the work, Sam and Rebekah sent their son to a private school in San Marcos, about thirty miles from Johnson City. Within a week of his arrival, Lyndon had bought so much ice cream and candy for his friends that he had spent all the pocket money Sam had given him for the entire eight-week course. When he hitchhiked home to ask for more money, Sam took him right back to San Marcos without giving him another penny.

Eventually, Lyndon Johnson began to emerge as a leader among students— certainly not in academics or in extracurricular activities, but by the force of his personality. "If there was an argument, he had to win," recalled Emmette Redford, who grew up with Johnson. "If he'd differ with you, he'd hover right up against you, breathing right in your face, arguing your point with all the earnestness...I got disgusted with him. Sometimes I'd try just to walk away, but...he wouldn't stop until you gave in."

His talent for arguing led Lyndon to join the debating club at Johnson City High School. It was one of the few extracurricular activities in which Lyndon would participate. In 1921, at the age of thirteen, he won his first debating contest, when he placed first in a meet in Fredericksburg for a speech titled "Texas: Undivided and Indivisible," a response to a persistent proposal by local politicians to split up the vast state into several smaller states. As a high school student, his skills earned him a trip to the finals of a debating competition in San Marcos. When he lost the competition, he was so distraught by the judges' decision that he threw up in the men's room.

Back at Johnson City High School, he was no more interested in academics than he had been in elementary school. The exception was civics class. By the time Lyndon took high school civics he already knew far more about how government worked than most boys his age. For years, Lyndon had sat on the front porch of the Johnson City home listening to Sam Johnson and his political cronies gossip about affairs in Austin. His high school civics class was taught by Scott Klett, who had attended law school at the University of Texas and was, therefore, far more educated than most everyone else

His talent for arguing led Lyndon to join the debating club at Johnson City High School.

The High School Department
OF THE
Johnson City Public School
ASSISTED BY MRS. S. E. JOHNSON
PRESENTS THE PLAY
"An Old Fashioned Mother"
THURSDAY NIGHT, MAY 3RD, 1923.

CAST OF CHARACTERS.

Deborah Underhill .... A Mother in Israel
    Annie Rae Ottmers.
Widder Bill Pindle... .. ..Leader of the Choir
    Georgia Cammack.
Miss Lowizy Loviny Custard .... Plain Sewing and Gossip
    Louise Casparis.
Isabel Simpscott.................The Village Belle
    Kittie Clyde Ross.
Gloriana Perkins ....As Good as Gold
    Margaret Johnson.
Sukey Pindle ... .The Widder's Mite
    Josefa Johnson.
John Underhill.................The Prodigal Son
    Lyndon Johnson.
Charley Underhill .... The Elder Brother
    Garland Galloway.
Brother Jonah Quackenbush....... ....A Whited Sepulchre
    John Dollahite.
Jeremiah Gosling, "Jerry".. ....A Merry Heart
    Truman Fawcett.
Enoch Rone ....An Outcast and a Wanderer
    Cecil Redford.
Quintus Todd.....................The County Sheriff
    Charley Hunnicutt.
The Village Choir.

Time: Twenty years ago. Place: The village of Canton in Northern New York.

SYNOPSIS.

ACT I—Settin' Room at the Underhill Farmhouse. An afternoon in late March. The Good Samaritan.

ACT II—Same scene, three years later. A winter afternoon. A Mother's Love.

ACT III—Same scene, two years later. A morning in autumn. The Prodigal Son.

ADMISSION, 15C AND 25C

Program, Johnson City High School Senior Play, *An Old Fashioned Mother*, 1923. Lyndon Johnson played "John Underhill, the Prodigal Son."

in town. Lyndon was fascinated by the lessons on government that he learned in Klett's class. Johnson City was also the seat of government of Blanco County, which meant the courthouse was located in the center of town. Recalled Emmette Redford: "There wasn't anything in town except three churches and a courthouse, and although Lyndon and I gave some attention to what was going on in the churches…we were more interested in what happened at the courthouse."

In 1920, the Johnson family fell on hard times when cotton prices suddenly dropped. The year before, Sam Johnson had gone heavily into debt to buy his parents' four-hundred-and-thirty-three-acre farm from his brothers and sisters. In 1919, cotton prices had risen to forty cents a pound. A year later, Sam Johnson's crop suffered from flooding in the winter and a hot spell in the summer. When a national recession and an international cotton surplus forced cotton prices to tumble to eight cents a pound, Sam was ruined. Even though he gave up his seat in the legislature and sold the farm, Sam still found himself drowning in bills that totaled $40,000—a debt that, after Sam's death in 1937, Lyndon and his brother and sisters would have to repay.

Johnson City High School only went up to the eleventh grade. What's more, the school was unaccredited, meaning that colleges did not regard its graduates as prepared to take their courses. In May 1924, Lyndon Johnson graduated from Johnson City High. His parents wanted him to attend Southwest Texas State Teachers College, but to enroll there that fall he would have to attend classes on the San Marcos campus over the summer, essentially taking twelfth-grade courses. Reluctantly, Lyndon enrolled, but lasted just a few weeks. He bristled under the workload and didn't believe he was up to the challenge. "Going to school as just another poor boy—well, that wasn't something Lyndon wanted to do," said his cousin, Elizabeth Roper Clemens.

Meanwhile, he continued his hell-raising ways. Not yet sixteen years old, Lyndon had started drinking. Despite Prohibition—the federal law that made alcoholic beverages illegal—Lyndon and his friends found ways to buy liquor, which they drank until they were drunk. They drove recklessly around Blanco County, daring the local sheriffs to chase them. Once, they burned down a barn. Said his grandmother, Ruth Baines: "That boy is going to end up in the penitentiary—just mark my words."

Instead of going to prison, Lyndon went to California. That July, Lyndon and four friends climbed into a beat-up Model T Ford and headed west. Lyndon's friends decided to look for jobs in California. Lyndon wasn't sure what he would do when he got there and planned on staying for just a few weeks. Instead, he spent two years in California, finding a job as a clerk in a San Bernardino law practice headed by a cousin, Tom Martin.

Martin promised to teach Lyndon the law, but it soon became clear that cousin Tom was managing to stay just a step ahead of the law himself. Martin was a drunk who rarely showed up in the office. Whenever Lyndon managed to contact

In May 1924, Lyndon Johnson completed the eleventh and final grade at Johnson City High School. This photograph shows members of the school's junior and senior classes. Not yet sixteen, Johnson was the youngest member of the class; he is in the back row, fifth from left.

his cousin with a question on how to handle a matter for a client, Martin told the young clerk to take care of the problem himself. Lyndon did the best he could, but was concerned that he could be in trouble with authorities for practicing law without a license. When Martin stopped paying Lyndon, he was forced to take a job as an elevator operator. Finally, in the fall of 1926, Lyndon returned home to Johnson City. His parents pressed him to go to college, but again he refused. Sam pulled some strings and found his son a job on a Texas Highway Department road crew. That was the job Lyndon held until the following February, when he argued with his boss and then said the wrong thing at the wrong time to a Fredericksburg farm boy with, as his cousin Ava recalled, "fists like a pile-driver."

After committing himself to attend college, Lyndon Johnson was one of 700 students matriculating at Southwest Texas State Teachers College when he arrived on campus in March 1927 to begin his college education. Although he would eventually become an honor student, at first Lyndon had no more interest in his studies than he had displayed in high school. Still, Lyndon aimed to make the best of his college experience.

Most of his fellow students came from backgrounds similar to Lyndon's—they were from small Texas towns in Hill Country, and most of them were from

Lyndon Johnson attended Southwest Texas State Teachers College at San Marcos from March 1927 to August 1930. Known as San Marcos, this small provincial school had little standing in the world of higher education. It opened in 1903 as a state "normal school" to train public school teachers. It became an accredited four-year college in 1925.

In this December 13, 1929, letter to his mother Rebekah Baines, Johnson describes the courses he registered for at San Marcos. "My schedule of classes is as follows: English 119—(a course in journalism) History 225 (American Diplomacy), Education 222 (a course in statistics), Education 252 (Practice Teaching), Religion (a study of the life of Jesus)," he wrote. "My courses this term have been unusually hard. They have required a great deal of application but the reward that application brings far overshadows the time spent. This has been my best college year."

poor families. As so-called "scholarship students," they held jobs on campus to help pay their way. Lyndon's first job was collecting trash—a chore he shared with several other students, most of whom complained about the work. Not Lyndon. Unlike the other students, Lyndon saw that there were better jobs on campus and understood the way to land one of the more desirable jobs was to impress the people who gave out the work. Lyndon went about picking up the trash with such unabashed zeal that he soon won a promotion to janitor's assistant. He spent just a short time in that job, landing a much-desired appointment as messenger in the office of Cecil Evans, the college president.

Lyndon had no intention of stopping there, either. Instead of simply carrying messages from building to building, Lyndon took on other duties in Evans' office: answering phones, announcing the arrival of visitors, and, after a brief time, acting as an appointment secretary for the president. Evans was grateful for the help and soon found himself relying on Lyndon, even taking him to Austin whenever he had business in the state capital. As the son of a former legislator, Lyndon knew many of the Texas lawmakers as well as the legislature's staff members, and he often used those contacts to steer Evans to people who could help the college.

In class, Lyndon excelled in debating, as he had done in high school. He grew close to Harry Greene, a political science professor and coach of the debating team, and would often spend hours at the end of each day with Greene, engaging his mentor in long-winded dialogues.

Although he had made himself into an influential member of the president's staff and had made a good friend on the faculty, Lyndon was still far from the center of student power on campus. A great deal of power was held by the leaders of the Black Stars, a campus fraternity that controlled the membership on the Student Council and, therefore, the flow of some $12,000 of the college's money into student activities. The problem was, though, that since the Black Stars were made up of athletes, most of the money went to the athletic teams. The school newspaper, literary magazine, music club, debating society, and other groups received few dollars from the Black Stars–led Student Council. Lyndon attempted to join the Black Stars but was rejected because he wasn't an athlete. So, Lyndon resolved to form a rival group, which he called the White Stars, and aimed to use his group to wrest control of the purse strings from the Black Stars.

It took three years. Lyndon's strategy was to slowly build up membership in the White Stars and run opposition slates for Student Council seats. In the first year, the White Stars won five seats on the council and took control of the student newspaper and literary magazine. Lyndon himself assumed the editorship of the paper, the *College Star*. During the second year, he used his influence to help assign jobs to the scholarship students. Relying on the old political patronage technique of awarding jobs to supporters, Lyndon gave the jobs in the library, bookstore, and administrative offices to White Stars supporters. Backers of the Black Stars were assigned to pick up the trash.

The final step toward taking control of the campus occurred in Lyndon's third and final year in San Marcos. Lyndon realized that to control the Student Council completely, the White Stars would have to elect the council president. Lyndon decided not to run himself; he believed his three-year effort to squash the Black Stars had made him too many enemies on campus. Instead, he convinced his best friend, Bill Deason, to run for president. The Black Stars slated their own candidate: Dick Speer, one of the most popular boys on campus.

Lyndon launched a relentless campaign for Deason. He organized teams of campaign workers to fan out across campus to round up support for the White Stars candidate. The White Stars worked for weeks, but the night before the vote a head count showed Deason still twenty votes behind Speer. The White Stars caucused to look over the poll numbers and most of them, including Deason, concluded that the election was out of reach. Lyndon wouldn't hear of defeat, however. He told the other White Stars: "The rest of you may go to bed, but I'm not." Lyndon headed out into the cold and drizzly Texas night. He went from boarding house to boarding house on campus, getting in people's faces, twisting arms, and making promises. Lyndon Johnson drew from all his talents as a debater to persuade ironclad Black Stars supporters to change their minds. "His greatest forte," Deason would later comment, "is to look a man in the eye and do a convincing job of selling him his viewpoint." When the votes were counted the next day, Deason was declared the winner by eight votes.

The Deason campaign was the beginning of a political career for Lyndon Johnson that would soon take him to Washington as a member of the U.S. House of Representatives (first elected in 1937) and then the Senate (first elected in 1949). In 1951, Johnson was elected the majority whip. In 1953, Johnson used all his political skills to convince his fellow Democratic senators to elect him minority leader. In 1954, when Democrats won control of the Senate, Johnson found himself majority leader—one of the most powerful jobs in the U.S. government.

In the midst of building a political career, Johnson found time to have a family. In 1934, he married Claudia Alta Taylor. Johnson called her "Lady Bird," a nickname she had been given as a small child by a nursemaid. The Johnsons would raise two daughters.

After losing the Democratic presidential nomination in 1960, Lyndon Johnson joined John F. Kennedy on the national ticket, winning election as vice president in November 1960. When Kennedy was assassinated in 1963, Johnson took the oath of office as president. A year later, "LBJ" was elected president to his own four-year term in a landslide victory.

As president, Johnson aimed to wipe out poverty in the United States. He signed legislation creating educational, medical, and housing programs for poor people, pledging to "build a great society, a place where the meaning of a man's life matches the marvels of man's labor." He also signed legislation ensuring civil rights to minorities, ending the decades-old practice of prohibiting African Americans

Transcript of Lyndon Johnson's grades at Southwest Texas State Teachers College. In August 1930, Lyndon Johnson received his B.S. degree in Education and History from Southwest Texas State Teachers College. "I never worked so hard in all my life," Johnson said later.

and other minorities from using restaurants, restrooms, train stations, and other public facilities that had been reserved for "whites only." And Johnson was a vigorous supporter of space exploration; during his presidency, he fully backed manned space travel, clearing the way for the first lunar landing in 1969. Despite these social advancements, Johnson's presidency will always be shadowed by the Vietnam War and his decision to escalate U.S. involvement in the conflict.

In the spring of 1968, Johnson shocked the nation when he announced on national television that he would not seek reelection. Johnson soon retired to his ranch near Johnson City. He died on January 22, 1973.

—Hal Marcovitz

Richard M. Nixon
Chapter Thirty-six

As he would often remind people during his years in public service, Richard Milhous Nixon was born into a poor, hardworking family. Yet the Nixon family valued education. Though he graduated from high school in the depths of the Great Depression, a combination of hard work, determination, and the support of his family gave Richard the opportunity for both a college education and a post-graduate degree.

The families of both of Richard Nixon's parents were deeply rooted in America. On his father's side, he was descended from James Nixon, who had arrived in Delaware from Ireland during the 1700s. On his mother's side, Franklin Milhous had immigrated to Pennsylvania from Germany—by way of England and Ireland—in 1729. Members of the Nixon family had served in both the American Revolution and the Civil War.

Richard Nixon was born on January 9, 1913, in a house that had been built by his father. He joined a family that included his father, Francis "Frank" Nixon; his mother, Hannah Milhous Nixon; and older brother Harold, born in 1909. A year later, Frank and Hannah Nixon had a third son, Francis Donald Nixon. Their early years were filled with hardship. Frank owned an orchard, but this business was not nearly as fruitful as he had hoped. Times were tough and it proved difficult to make ends meet. The business venture failed in 1922, two years after a fourth child, Arthur, was born. Frank Nixon sold the house in Yorba Linda, California, and moved his family to Whittier. Here, Frank opened a gas station to which a grocery store was soon attached. Though it was a demanding enterprise, this business eventually achieved modest success.

The young Nixons had started school in Yorba Linda, but Harold and Richard transferred to East Whittier Elementary in 1922 when Richard was in the fourth grade. Much of their education, however, came from their parents and from the social and religious life within the large Quaker community in Whittier. The family attended Quaker services at least twice a week, and young Richard served as the church organist when he was still in grade school.

Richard Nixon is seated in the front row, extreme right, in this 1919 photograph of his first grade class, Yorba Linda, California.

"I started first grade in Yorba Linda's schoolhouse when I was six," Nixon wrote in his *Memoirs* (1978). "My mother had already taught me to read at home, and this head start enabled me to skip the second grade. After homework and chores, I often sat by the fireplace or at the kitchen table immersed in a book or magazine. We took the *Los Angeles Times*, the *Saturday Evening Post*, and the *Ladies' Home Journal*. Aunt Olive, my mother's youngest sister, and her husband, Oscar Marshburn, lived in nearby Whittier and subscribed to the *National Geographic*. Nearly every time I visited them I borrowed a copy. It was my favorite magazine."

Nixon was not a boy who enjoyed pranks. "He was very mature even when he was five or six years old," his mother Hannah Nixon recalled in a 1960 interview. "He was interested in things way beyond the usual grasp of a boy his age. He was thoughtful and serious. 'He always carried such a weight.' That's an expression we Quakers use for a person who doesn't take his responsibilities lightly."

Much of Nixon's education came from his parents and from the social and religious life within the large Quaker community in Whittier.

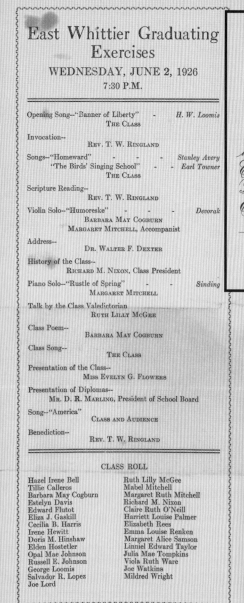

East Whittier Graduating Exercises

WEDNESDAY, JUNE 2, 1926
7:30 P.M.

Opening Song--"Banner of Liberty" - H. W. Loomis
THE CLASS

Invocation--
REV. T. W. RINGLAND

Songs--"Homeward" - Stanley Avery
"The Birds' Singing School" - Earl Towner
THE CLASS

Scripture Reading--
REV. T. W. RINGLAND

Violin Solo--"Humoreske" - Devorak
BARBARA MAY COGBURN
MARGARET MITCHELL, Accompanist

Address--
DR. WALTER F. DEXTER

History of the Class--
RICHARD M. NIXON, Class President

Piano Solo--"Rustle of Spring" - Sinding
MARGARET MITCHELL

Talk by the Class Valedictorian
RUTH LILLY MCGEE

Class Poem--
BARBARA MAY COGBURN

Class Song--
THE CLASS

Presentation of the Class--
MISS EVELYN G. FLOWERS

Presentation of Diplomas--
MR. D. R. MARLING, President of School Board

Song--"America"
CLASS AND AUDIENCE

Benediction--
REV. T. W. RINGLAND

CLASS ROLL

Hazel Irene Bell	Ruth Lilly McGee
Tillie Calleros	Mabel Mitchell
Barbara May Cogburn	Margaret Ruth Mitchell
Estelyn Davis	Richard M. Nixon
Edward Flutot	Claire Ruth O'Neill
Eliza J. Gaskill	Harriett Louise Palmer
Cecilia B. Harris	Elizabeth Rees
Irene Hewitt	Emma Louise Renken
Doris M. Hinshaw	Margaret Alice Samson
Elden Hostetler	Linniel Edward Taylor
Opal Mae Johnson	Julia Mae Tompkins
Russell E. Johnson	Viola Ruth Ware
George Loomis	Joe Watkins
Salvador R. Lopez	Mildred Wright
Joe Lord	

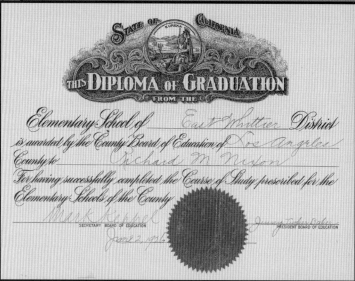

A program for the East Whittier Elementary School graduating exercises, held on June 2, 1926, and Nixon's elementary school diploma.

Richard Nixon was a conscientious student. A classmate recalled, "Dick very seldom came out and played. He was usually studying, and there were remarks and cracks made about it." Another classmate remembered, "He was a little different from the rest of us. He was a kid you respected. He knew everyone, but he was very good in class, and when you talked to him you always had his full attention. He was friendly, but not a guy you'd put on a backpack and go fishing with."

There were twenty-nine students in Nixon's eighth grade class. He was the class president and delivered a brief talk on the "History of the Class."

The Nixon boys would also learn early the value of hard work. They were pressed into service to help out at Frank Nixon's store, and they spent their school vacations doing farm work to add cash to the Nixon family coffers.

At home, Richard Nixon's parents were a study in contrasts. Hannah Nixon was a kind, gentle, and thoughtful woman whom Richard would later often refer to as "a saint." Frank Nixon, on the other hand, was an outspoken and often angry man. His anger came from the fact that he was a barely educated laborer battling to succeed while competing with more established businessmen. While Hannah was a serene influence on the home, Frank often went off on frightening tirades.

Frank Nixon was not, however, irrational in his ranting and raving. His opinions were generally well reasoned and supported by facts. From his father, Richard learned to debate, but he also learned the value of knowing facts that would sustain his points of view. To gain these facts, Richard became an avid newspaper reader when he was still in grade school. Thanks to his father's inspiration, and to his own study and hard work, Richard emerged as an accomplished debater in an era when public debates were seen as a form of entertainment. His first debate before an audience—on the merits of renting versus owning real estate—set the stage for his future behind a podium as a political figure.

Just as he inherited his father's skill as a debater, Richard inherited much of his father's bitterness. The years of poverty and struggle, both before and after the orchard business failed, had made a deep impression on him. He would develop an appreciation for diligence and hard work, but on the dark side, he also resented people of privilege who seemed to have wealth handed to them. Like Frank Nixon, Richard developed an inferiority complex that would affect his outlook for the rest of his life. In high school, when he drove a delivery truck for his father, Richard was so ashamed to be doing this kind of work that he went out of his way to not be seen in the truck by his classmates.

Richard entered high school in the fall of 1926 in nearby Fullerton, but transferred to Whittier High School for his junior and senior years. Despite having to work in all of his spare time, he was an above-average student. He joined the debate team and soon became one of its stars. Though he was bashful and withdrawn around small groups of fellow students, he had no fear of speaking to crowds. As a result, he became a prizewinning orator and honed important skills as a public speaker that would be vital in his later career.

His time in high school was bracketed by two of the most tragic events that a young person could experience—the death of two siblings. His seven-year-old brother Arthur became sick in August 1925, just as Richard was entering the eighth grade. Doctors were unable to find a cause for his illness and he died a few weeks later. Then, about the time he graduated from Whittier High School in 1930, Richard found out that his older brother Harold had been diagnosed with tuberculosis, a widely feared and often deadly respiratory disease. Treatment at a sanitarium in the dry air of northern Arizona was recommended, and Harold was hospitalized at an institution in Prescott. Hannah Nixon moved to Arizona to be with her son, and wound up working on the janitorial staff to help pay his bills. Two years later, in March 1933, Harold passed away.

The early 1930s were trying times for the Nixon family. Harold was ill, Hannah was away from the rest of the family, and family finances were stretched thin. This already-difficult situation was complicated by the fact that Frank and Hannah had a late-in-life fifth son in 1930. Little Edward Nixon arrived in the world just as the Nixons' next-youngest son, Francis Donald, was turning sixteen and as Richard was graduating from high school.

In the meantime, Richard had been accepted to Whittier College, a Quaker institution in his hometown that his mother had attended. This was all the Nixons could afford. Though he had also applied for scholarships to prestigious Ivy League schools back east, including Harvard and Yale, the family situation clearly made it impossible for him to leave home. He started classes in the fall of 1930 and lived at home to help out with household chores while his father cared for the new baby.

Young Richard Nixon's character had been forged in adversity and shaped by tragedy. In college, he developed a reputation as a serious student. He appeared so somber to many fellow students that he would eventually earn the nickname "Gloomy Gus."

Despite this, his talent for public speaking made him a well-known campus figure at Whittier. It might be said that while everyone came to know him, few people knew him well. He was elected president of his freshman class and he became co-founder, with his friend Dean Triggs, of a new fraternity that was known as the Orthogonian Society.

One can clearly see Nixon's influence in the founding principles of the Orthogonians. The society was created as a reaction to the Franklin Society, a group of men who wore tuxedos and fancied themselves as being "upper crust." It was here that Nixon's resentment of the wealthy upper class came out. He imagined himself as a "common man." Orthogonians wore open-necked shirts and were deliberately informal. Most of the members, like Nixon, were working their way through school. Orthogonians were self-described as "square shooters"—men who said what they meant and did not hide behind pretense. For much of his career, Nixon would characterize himself as such a person.

Though just a freshman, Richard Milhous Nixon was elected as the first president of the Orthogonians. He even penned the lyrics to the fraternity's song, which closes with the phrase, "Brothers together we'll travel on and on, worthy of the name of Orthogonian." The Orthogonian Society remains at Whittier College to this day.

When he was a sophomore, Nixon joined the debate team. Just as he had in high school, he emerged as a renowned debater, and he won numerous intercollegiate contests for Whittier College. He also went out for football. He made the team, but was not nearly so skilled on the field as behind the podium. As a result, he spent most of his brief pigskin career on the bench. Nevertheless, he was to be greatly influenced by Coach Wallace Newman, who Nixon recalled as having been an inspiration to the young men, teaching them important life skills, such as honesty and fair play, as he was teaching them plays.

On the academic side, Nixon was an excellent student. Math and science were a challenge for him, but he breezed through history, studying under the esteemed history professor Paul Smith.

Perhaps his most influential teacher at Whittier College was Albert Upton, professor of English and literature. An expert in Aristotelian logic, Upton was

Nixon said that he had two unfulfilled ambitions—to direct a symphony orchestra and to play an organ in a cathedral.

Richard Nixon loved music. He began to play the piano before he was five years of age. Nixon said that he had two unfulfilled ambitions—to direct a symphony orchestra and to play an organ in a cathedral. During a concert that was part of his 1969 presidential inauguration ceremony, as pianist Andre Watts was playing, Nixon's aunt leaned over and whispered to the President, "Now Richard. If thee had practiced more on the piano, thee could have been down there instead of up here!"

Nixon is in the back row standing, second from the right in this 1929 photograph of the Fullerton High School orchestra.

Richard Nixon (back row, third from left) with the other members of the Whittier High School debating team, circa 1930. At Whittier High, Nixon joined a myriad of clubs—the Latin Club, the school newspaper, the school orchestra, the football team, and the debating team. Mrs. Clifford Vincent (front row, center), the teacher/coach of the debating team, recalled, "He was so good it kind of disturbed me. He had the ability to kind of slide round an argument instead of meeting it head on, and he could take any side of a debate."

Program

Presiding: John F. D. Aue, Managing Editor, Whittier News.

Selection—Prince of Pilsen . . . . *Luders*

The Stars and Stripes Forever . . . . *John Philip Sousa*
Whittier Union High School Orchestra

Address of Welcome:
Mr. O. C. Albertson, District Superintendent
Whittier Union High School District

———

ORATIONS:

1. The Constitution and the Duty of the Citizens . . . . *Helen Cox*
2. Our Privileges Under the Constitution . . . . . *Richard Nixon*
3. The Constitution, its Contribution to World Peace *Leland Klingerman*
4. The Individual, His Rights and Duties Under
   the Constitution . . . . *Karl Von der Ahe*
5. Our Constitution—Practical and Ideal . . . . . . *Hilla Willard*
6. The Constitution in the Upbuilding of the United States *Henry Meyers*
7. The Vitality of the Constitution . . . . *Robert McArthur*

———

Come to the Fair . . . . *Easthope-Martin*

Nightfall in Granada . . . . *L. Baeno*
Whittier Union High School

———

A loving cup donated by Whittier Union High School will be presented to the winner.

JUDGES:

Hon. Leon R. Yankwich, Judge of the Superior Court, Los Angeles.

Mr. W. C. Hay, President, Blue Diamond Company, Los Angeles.

Mr. Wm. Carey Marble, President, The John C. Marble Company, Los Angeles.

Georgia P. Bullock, Judge of the Municipal Court, Los Angeles.

Hon. Walter S. Gates, Judge of the Superior Court, Los Angeles.

———

PACIFIC COAST GRAND FINALS

On Friday evening, May 10th, at the Shrine Civic Auditorium, Los Angeles, the winning orators representing Arizona, California, Idaho, Nevada, Oregon, Utah, Washington and the Territory of Hawaii will compete for the right to represent this section in the National Finals to be held at Washington, D. C., on May 25th. The Chief Justices of the Supreme Courts of the states concerned will be present to act as judges for the event. A presiding officer of national prominence has been secured. A combined band from the High Schools of the City of Los Angeles will furnish music for the occasion. There will be no charge for admission. Reservations for seats for the Pacific Coast Finals may be had by writing Alan Nichols, Contest Director, Oratorical Contest Department, Los Angeles Times.

In the spring of 1929, sixteen-year-old Richard Nixon entered an area-wide oratorical contest sponsored by the *Los Angeles Times*. The subject was the Constitution of the United States. Nixon called his speech "Our Privileges Under the Constitution." He won the contest. These pages are from Nixon's program for the contest.

Nixon attended Fullerton High School in his freshman and sophomore years and Whittier High School for his junior and senior years. After graduating from high school in 1930, young Nixon, whom his class had voted "best all-around student," was awarded a scholarship to Harvard University. But he could not take advantage of this educational opportunity, because his family could not afford to pay his traveling and living expenses.

highly regarded for his theories involving fundamental thinking processes based on semantics, cognitive psychology, and problem solving. He greatly influenced the future president by defining the conceptualization, qualification, and classification of language. From Upton, Nixon would learn a great deal about analyzing and solving problems.

As a senior, Nixon was elected student-body president, a crowning achievement to his campus career. In 1934, he graduated summa cum laude and second in his class with a bachelor's degree in history.

His academic success at Whittier earned Nixon a scholarship to the Duke University Law School in Durham, North Carolina. At Duke, Nixon avoided campus politics until his senior year, concentrating on his studies and on part-time jobs that he took to help out with expenses. These included work in the campus library and at the National Youth Administration. Academically, he received praise for a 1936 term paper in legal ethics that was entitled, "Automobile Accident Litigation: The lawyer versus the public." Again, his interests were colored by his image of himself as a common man and as a champion of underdogs.

As a senior, he was elected president of the Duke Bar Association, and he joined the honorary legal fraternity known as the Order of the Coif. In June 1937, Richard Nixon graduated third in his class of twenty-five with a Bachelor of Laws degree.

While at Duke, Nixon had decided that he would like to pursue a career with the Federal Bureau of Investigation. His application was turned down, so he returned to Southern California to practice law. He was admitted to the California bar in the autumn of 1937, and he joined the Whittier law firm of Wingert & Bewley. The firm had as one of its clients the city government of La Habra, California, a small city about halfway between Whittier and Yorba Linda.

Nixon set up a branch office in La Habra for Wingert & Bewley, and he soon became a full partner in the firm (renamed Bewley, Knoop, & Nixon). In La Habra, Nixon found himself performing a variety of tasks. He might be doing tax work one day and in court on a criminal case the next. It was a diverse career for the young attorney.

In 1940, Nixon was named to the board of trustees of his alma mater, Whittier College, a post that he would retain until 1968, the year he was elected president of the United States. In his spare time between 1937 and 1940, Nixon joined an amateur theater troupe, and it was here that he met a young schoolteacher named Thelma Catherine Patricia "Pat" Ryan. Pat Ryan and Richard Nixon were married on June 21, 1940.

Nixon had planned to apply for a job at a larger law firm, possibly in Los Angeles. However, in 1941, shortly before the United States entered World War II, the Nixons moved to Washington, D.C., where Richard Nixon took a government job as an attorney with the Office of Price Administration. After the

Japanese attack on Pearl Harbor and the subsequent U.S. declaration of war in December 1941, Nixon applied to join the armed forces. He earned a commission as a lieutenant, junior grade, in the U.S. Naval Reserve on June 15, 1942. He went on active duty two months later, and was sent for aviation training at the Naval Training School at Quonset Point, Rhode Island.

Beginning in May 1943 Nixon served in the South Pacific with the Combat Air Transport Command at Guadalcanal. In December 1944, Nixon, now a full lieutenant, was assigned to the Navy Bureau of Aeronautics office in Washington, D.C. He served for four months at the Navy Department offices in the nation's capital, and was then transferred to the Bureau of Aeronautics as an officer in the contract termination office. Though he was based in New York City, his work took him to various cities on the East Coast.

Richard Nixon left active duty with the navy in March 1946, and he and Pat returned to California. They had been lured back, in part, by a group of Republican businessmen who had asked Nixon whether he'd like to go into politics. If so, they said they would be willing to finance his run for the Twelfth District seat in the U.S. House of Representatives that had been held for five terms by a Democrat named Horace Jeremiah "Jerry" Voorhis. Nixon agreed to take up the challenge of running for office.

During the campaign, it was suggested that Voorhis, who had socialist leanings, was a communist sympathizer. In 1946, in Southern California, there was little sympathy for communist sympathizers. Nixon handily won the election, in part because of the communism issue and in part because of his skills in debate and public speaking.

In Washington, Nixon was assigned to the House Un-American Activities Committee. It was here that he would make a name for himself during the committee's investigation of a former State Department aide named Alger Hiss, who was accused of being a communist subversive. Nixon would soon rise to national prominence, nurturing the image of himself as a tireless crusader against communism.

Though he was easily reelected to Congress in 1948, Nixon had larger ambitions. In 1950, California had an open seat in the U.S. Senate, and Nixon decided to run for that office. His Democratic opponent was Helen Gahagan Douglas, a former actress and the wife of Hollywood leading man Melvyn Douglas, who had already served three terms in the House of Representatives. Touring the state in a station wagon equipped with a public address system, Nixon stated his case to voters. He built on his reputation as an anti-communist by accusing his opponent of communist leanings. Also during the 1950 campaign, Nixon turned his long-held disdain for the rich and privileged into a useful campaign tool. Because the Douglases were seen as wealthy, Nixon was able to paint his opponent as being "out of touch" with the "common man." Douglas, who considered Nixon's campaign tactics to be unfair and underhanded, coined the nickname "Tricky Dick" for her opponent, an epithet that would be continually resurrected for the rest of his

Friend's College, Whittier, Cal. 633

Richard Nixon attended Whittier College from 1930 to 1934. Whittier had about four hundred students. More than half had graduated from the town high school and most, like Nixon, lived at home. "I was not disappointed," Nixon recalled, "because the idea of college was so exciting that nothing could have dimmed it for me."

The postcard above shows the school as it appeared around 1930, when Nixon arrived on campus. The school had been started as Friends Academy in 1887. By 1930, it was nonsectarian but, as its catalogue stated, was "devoted to higher education with a constant overtone of Quaker responsibility in the social order." Of the eighty-five graduates in Nixon's class of 1934, only twelve settled out of state and more than twenty lived their lives within walking distance of the college.

political career. Despite being characterized as a trickster, Nixon saw his victory in the hard-fought 1950 election as that of an underdog triumphing over adversity.

After two years in the Senate, Nixon went on to serve two terms as vice president under President Dwight D. Eisenhower, from 1953 to 1961. In 1960, he ran unsuccessfully for president against John F. Kennedy, losing one of the closest elections in history. Two years later, hoping to recapture the magic of his successful congressional campaigns, he ran against incumbent California governor Edmund G. "Pat" Brown. When Nixon lost the 1962 gubernatorial race, he was bitter. He told a television audience that he was quitting politics forever—"You won't have Dick Nixon to kick around anymore."

Despite this promise, Nixon returned to the national stage six years later with a successful 1968 campaign for president, in which he defeated Democrat

"Ever since I first played in high school, football has been my favorite sport," Nixon recalled in his *Memoirs*. "As a 150-pound seventeen-year-old freshman I hardly cut a formidable figure on the field, but I loved the game—the spirit, the teamwork, the friendship. There were only eleven eligible men on the freshman team, so despite my size and weight I got to play in every game and to wear a number on my sweater. But for the rest of my college years, the only times I got to play were in the last few minutes of a game that was already safely won or hopelessly lost."

Nixon is in the back row, center, in this 1931 photograph of part of the Whittier College football team.

Richard Nixon (top row, fifth from left) and his Duke University Law School Class, 1937.

"One day during my last year at Whittier," wrote Nixon, "I saw a notice on the bulletin board announcing twenty-five $250 scholarships to the new Duke University Law School in Durham, North Carolina. I applied."

Hannah Nixon said that the proudest day of her life was when the letter arrived stating her son had won a scholarship—"yes, even prouder than the day Richard became Vice President."

"I was able to maintain the grades I needed to keep my scholarship and I became a member of Duke's law review," wrote Nixon. "My three years at Duke provided an excellent legal background."

Hubert Humphrey. Nixon was reelected in 1972 by a wide margin, but almost immediately found himself embroiled in the Watergate scandal. As reports of presidential misconduct grew, Nixon ultimately decided to resign the presidency on August 9, 1974.

It is unfortunate that today the reputation of President Richard Milhous Nixon is shaded by the dark cloud of Watergate. In his early life, Nixon's character seems to have been quite the opposite of the chief executive who sanctioned a criminal cover-up. If any lesson can be drawn from the sad climax of Nixon's career, it is how a serious misdeed can undo the positive results of a life of hard work and dedication.

—Bill Yenne

Gerald Ford
Chapter Thirty-seven

The University of Michigan can usually be counted on to field one of the nation's best college football teams. That has not always been the case. In the fall of 1934, the team was crippled by the loss of many of its most talented players through the previous spring's graduation. The players who remained on the team were young and inexperienced, and it soon became clear that Michigan's varsity was outclassed by most of its opponents. The Wolverines lost their first two games that season, falling in each contest by lopsided scores.

As the team prepared for its third game, against Georgia Tech, the Wolverines found themselves faced with another problem. One of the team's best players was Willis F. Ward, an African-American track star who played pass receiver. In the 1930s, black athletes were just beginning to be accepted onto college campuses in the northern states. That was not true in the still-segregated South. As the game with Georgia Tech approached, administrators from the southern school made it clear their team would refuse to take the field if Ward played.

Michigan coach Harry Kipke soon capitulated and ordered Ward to stay home for the Georgia Tech game. That decision sent a wave of anger through the Wolverine squad. One of the players most upset by Kipke's decision was Jerry Ford, the team's center. Ford had grown close to Ward because the two players roomed together during Michigan's road games. If Ward could not take the field, Ford told his friend, he would sit out the game as well. It was Ward who talked Jerry into playing. "Look," Ward told Jerry, "the team's having a bad year. We've lost two games already and we probably won't win any more. You've got to play Saturday. You owe it to the team."

Jerry changed his mind, deciding that the best way to react to Georgia Tech's racist attitude was on the field. That Saturday, Michigan played its best game of the season. Early in the game, one of the Georgia Tech players taunted the Michigan team for including a "nigger" on its squad. When play resumed a few minutes later, Ford laid such a savage block on that player that he had to be carried off the field on a stretcher. Michigan went on to win that day by a score of 9 to 2. It would be

Gerald R. Ford, the only president to become an Eagle Scout, holds the flag as he and his fellow members of the Eagle Scout Guard of Honor prepare to raise the colors over Fort Michilimackinac at Mackinac Island State Park, Michigan. This photograph was taken in August 1929. The troop served as guides for tourists during the summer months.

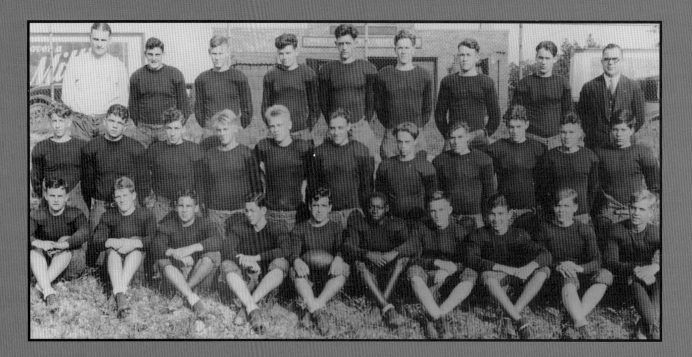

South High School football team, Grand Rapids, Michigan, 1930. Gerald Ford is in the second row, fifth from left. Clifford Gettings, upper left, was the coach. Many considered Gettings the most important faculty member at South High.

In his autobiography, Gerald Ford devotes more than fifty pages to his childhood and education. He mentions no book or teacher that had any influence on him, except Gettings. Ford did recall that "as a child I had a hot temper, which Mother taught me to control—most of the time. A strict disciplinarian, she would ridicule me and show me how foolish I looked when I got angry and said stupid things.... One time she gave me the poem 'If,' by Rudyard Kipling. 'Read this and profit from it,' she said. 'It'll help you control that temper of yours.'" Ford does not write whether he read this inspirational poem or if her advice had an effect upon his temper. Ford's recollection of his school years deals with the fierce competition and exultation of the football field.

Ford spent many hours speaking with his close friend Jerald F. terHorst about his early life and education. TerHorst, in his biography of the former president, mentions no book that Ford had read. Again, the emphasis is Ford's participation in sports.

Football was much more important in Grand Rapids when Ford was growing up during the 1920s than it is today. There were fewer competing attractions. There was no television. Very few students had an automobile available to them. Student social life focused on what one did after the Saturday afternoon football game. School district boundaries were fixed on a city region basis. School bussing did not exist. Football rivalry between high schools also involved neighborhood pride. And, the football coach, rather than the teaching staff, helped to determine the reputation of a school.

Football was the biggest influence on Ford's education. It brought him national attention as a teenager. His skill on the field enabled him to obtain a university education and a law degree. It enhanced his courtship of Betty Bloomer, who studied under the famous dancer Martha Graham, and who believed, as Ford did, in physical grace and fitness. In Ford's sophomore year at Grand Rapids South High School, he played center on the city championship football team. He was named to the All-city and All-state teams.

Ford's popularity extended beyond South High. In 1930, the Majestic Theater, the largest in downtown Grand Rapids, joined a midwestern promotional contest to identify the most popular high school senior in fifty participating cities. Theater patrons wrote their candidates' name on ballots and dropped them in lobby boxes. As the Grand Rapids winner, Ford traveled to Chicago where he met the boys and girls of the other cities. Then, it was a train trip to Washington, D.C., for five days of sight-seeing. Apparently, the future president drew no inspiration from the trip. "Ending up in Washington was just about the farthest thing from my mind," he wrote. "Back then I had absolutely no interest in politics or a career in government." Ford wanted to become a famous baseball player!

the only game that Michigan won that year, but for Jerry Ford and his teammates, it was perhaps the sweetest victory of their college careers.

Gerald R. Ford Jr., who would go on to become the nation's thirty-eighth president, was born in Omaha, Nebraska, on July 14, 1913. His name at birth was Leslie Lynch King Jr. His mother, Dorothy, divorced his father when the boy was two, taking him to her parents' home in Grand Rapids, Michigan. In Grand Rapids, she met and married Gerald R. Ford Sr., who adopted her son, gave him his name, and raised Jerry as his own. Over the years Jerry would have only brief contact with his biological father.

Dorothy and Gerald Ford Sr. would become the parents of three more sons— James, Richard, and Thomas Ford. The Fords were a close-knit family who met the challenges of life in Depression-era America through diligence, hard work, and a commitment to small-town values. Gerald Ford Sr. started his own paint company, which mostly sold its products to the many furniture factories located in Grand Rapids. During the Depression, Jerry's stepfather struggled to make a profit and the Fords often found themselves scrimping to make ends meet.

Jerry started kindergarten at Madison Elementary School in Grand Rapids in 1918. Even at that age, Jerry was athletic and loved sports. He recalled playing football and softball on the gravel playground behind the school building, and coming home with torn clothes and skinned knees. He spent just two years at Madison, and then enrolled in East Grand Rapids Elementary School when his family moved to a new home across town.

Jerry struggled with a stuttering problem as an elementary school student, but outgrew it by the age of ten. "Some words gave me fits and it was a struggle for me to get them out," Ford would later recall. "I don't know what caused the problem."

Although he cured his own stutter, Jerry soon confounded his teachers with a different sort of peculiarity—he was ambidextrous, meaning he could write and do other tasks with equal ability with either hand. "My parents and early teachers… became quite concerned and tried to make me use my right hand all the time. After a while, they gave up and I continued switching hands as I'd done before," he said.

By the time Jerry entered South High School in Grand Rapids, sports were an important part of his academic life. He competed on the baseball, basketball, and track teams, but his main sport was football. As a sophomore, he played center and linebacker on the South High School team that won the city championship. Even as a sophomore, his teammates looked to him as a leader.

Although he was a star athlete, Jerry was hardly anybody's idea of a "Big Man on Campus." He was quiet, did not date much, and was regarded by many of his fellow students as something of a square. Jerry was the only student at South High School who made it a point of wearing a suit and tie every day.

Jerry's performance in the classroom did not measure up to his achievements on the football field. Other than sports, Ford participated in few extracurricular activities at South High. He was a good student, earning solid B's in most subjects, but there were exceptions. He struggled with mathematics, usually able to attain only grades of C, but he excelled in history and political science, often earning A's. "Jerry and I were the best pupils in the class," Virginia Berry, Jerry's classmate in American history, later recalled. "Our teacher gave weekly exams and the way it went was one week I would get a 96 and Jerry a 93, next week he'd get a 97 and I'd get a 94. I sat in the back of the room and Jerry up front, and every time exams were returned he would come back to see what my grade was. He didn't resent if I got a better grade, he was just checking. We both got As in that subject, the only two in the class."

Well after his political career started, Jerry regretted not being a better student of English or speech in high school. "Nothing in life is more important than the ability to communicate effectively," he said.

In the fall of 1929 the American stock market crashed, sending the country into a deep economic depression. The family paint business suffered, and Jerry's stepfather was barely able to keep the business running. His employees agreed to work for pennies while he struggled to keep the plant in operation. The Fords felt the sting as much as anyone in town. Gerald Ford Sr. was no longer able to make the mortgage payments on the East Grand Rapids home. The bank took over the property, and the Fords were forced to move into a smaller home in another part of town.

By then, Jerry was a junior in high school. He was a star on the football team and participated in other

Gerald Ford's high school graduation picture, 1931.
"Athletics, my parents kept saying, built a boy's character," Ford recalled. "They were important, but not nearly as important as attaining good grades. My parents made sure that I did my homework and pressed me to excel. In chemistry and other science courses, I received average grades. In Latin, which I disliked, it was a struggle to earn C's. Math was not too difficult. In the courses I really enjoyed, history and government, I did very well."

These pages are from Gerald Ford's Grand Rapids South High School transcript.

Ford was elected to the National Honor Society at the end of his junior year (1930). The society, which had been established the previous year by the Association of Secondary School Principals, honored those students in their junior year who distinguished themselves in scholarship and in athletics.

Ford ranked in the top five percent of his two-hundred-and-twenty-member graduating class, with an overall grade average of 89.58 percent. Latin was his poorest subject, and history and physical training were his best subjects.

sports as well. The Fords' new home was several miles away from South High School. Instead of transferring to a closer high school, Jerry chose to finish his education at South High. This meant he had to rise early every morning to ride a bus into town, where he transferred to another bus that took him to South High. The ride each way took nearly an hour. Jerry didn't mind the ride to school, as it gave him an opportunity to study before class. But on the way home, Jerry was often weary from football practice and had to struggle to stay awake so he wouldn't fall asleep and miss his stop. Eventually, Jerry scraped together $75 that he had earned from part-time jobs and bought an old Model T Ford that he drove to school.

"The car ran beautifully during the football season, but then cold weather set in," Ford remembered. "One December day, the temperature fell below zero and there was snow on the ground. Because I didn't know much about cars, I hadn't bothered to pour antifreeze into the radiator. I parked the car at school, attended varsity basketball practice and drove home for dinner that night. As I pulled into the driveway, I noticed clouds of steam rising up from the engine. I lifted the hood, saw that the motor was a fiery red and decided, incredibly, that what I needed was something to keep the car warm all night. Some old blankets were lying in the garage. I laid them on top of the engine and went inside to eat. Just as we finished the family meal, we heard fire engine sirens loud and close. We looked out the window and my poor car was in flames." The hot engine had ignited the blankets

Jerry had placed on the hood to keep the car warm. The car was a total loss. Jerry hadn't bothered to buy insurance for the vehicle, so his entire investment of $75 went up in smoke. The next morning, he was back on the bus.

By the end of his senior year at South High, Jerry very much wanted to attend college but there was no way his parents could afford the tuition. Arthur Krause, the principal of South High School, arranged for Jerry to receive an athletic scholarship from the University of Michigan. The scholarship covered Jerry's tuition of $100 a year. By today's standards this would be a paltry sum for a college education, but for the Depression-era families in the 1930s it was well beyond most people's means.

The scholarship took care of the tuition, but there were other costs, such as books and room and board. Harry Kipke, the Michigan football coach, found Jerry a job waiting on tables in a university hospital dining room. An aunt and uncle promised to send him two dollars a week for pocket money. He arrived on campus in Ann Arbor in the fall of 1931. "So the hotshot center from Grand Rapids came to live at Michigan in a third-floor 10-by-10 room way in the back of the cheapest rooming house I could find," Ford said. "I shared the rent—$4 a week—with a basketball player. We each had a desk and a bed, which pretty much exhausted the floor space, and there was one small window between us."

Things did improve. Soon after enrolling at Michigan, Jerry joined the Delta Kappa Delta fraternity, and was able to move into a nicer room in the Deltas' fraternity house, although he had to work as a dishwasher to pay his rent. He majored in economics and political science. Again, his grades reflected the work of one who was certainly committed to his studies, although he hardly stood out academically. He finished with a B average, scoring A's in just four courses over his four-year college career: American government, economics, European history, and labor studies.

After the disappointing football season of 1934, Jerry finished his classes at Michigan in the spring of 1935 with little notion of what to do following graduation. He thought he would like to take up the study of law, but was aware that he could not afford tuition to a law school. His performance on the Wolverines' varsity football team prompted two football teams to make him offers to play professionally. The Detroit Lions and Green Bay Packers each offered him contracts to play for them in the fall of 1935, but in that era professional football was not the sport that it is today. It was considered a minor-league sport at the time, played in small stadiums before few fans. Each team offered him contracts that amounted to about $2,800 a year. Ford turned them down.

When Coach Kipke learned that the Yale University football team, coached by his friend Raymond "Ducky" Pond, was looking for an assistant coach, he contacted Pond and recommended Ford as a candidate. Pond invited Ford to visit the Yale campus in New Haven, Connecticut, to talk about the job. "Everywhere I went [at Yale], I discerned an atmosphere of scholarship, dignity, and tradition,"

This photograph shows Gerald Ford on the field of Michigan Stadium at the University of Michigan, Ann Arbor, 1933. Ford was a second-stringer until his senior year.

Ford graduated from South High School in 1931. His football achievements won him a scholarship to the University of Michigan. At Michigan, Ford was as popular as he had been in high school.

In 1934, Ford's final year on the football team, Michigan lost seven of its nine games. But, Ford's outstanding abilities as a center and linebacker won him an invitation to play in the East-West Shrine Game in San Francisco on January 1, 1935. (Pictured are the cover and pages from the game program.) Ford's fifty-eight minutes on the field were good enough to win him offers from the Green Bay Packers and the Detroit Lions to play professional football.

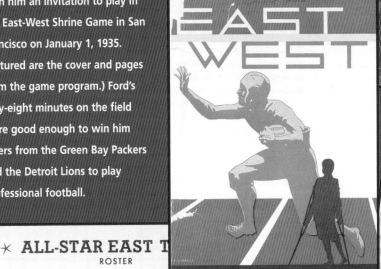

BENEFIT SHRINERS HOSPITAL
✶ FOR CRIPPLED CHILDREN

 ## ✶ ALL-STAR EAST TEAM ✶
ROSTER
✶

No.	Name	College	Position	Age	Weight	Home Town
5	Borden, Lester	Fordham	R. End	22	179	
10	Hartwig, Charles	U. of Pitt.	L. Guard	22	190	
11	Veller, Donald	Indiana	Quarter	22	158	
14	Steen, James	Syracuse	L. Tackle	21	200	New Rochelle, N.Y.
16	Munjas, Miller	U. of Pitt.	Quarter	23	185	Bellaire, O.
17	Weinstock, Isadore	U. of Pitt.	Fullback	21	198	Wilkes-Barre, Pa.
18	Brominski, Edward	Columbia	R. Half	22	171	Swoyerville, Pa.
21	Shepherd, William	Western Maryland	L. Half	23	185	Clearfield, Pa.
22	Leeper, Harry	Northwestern U.	L. End	21	186	Fort Wayne, Ind.
23	Ford, Gerald	U. of Michigan	Center	21	197	Grand Rapids, Mich.
33	Whalen, Edward	Northwestern U.	R. Guard	22	182	Chicago, Ill.
34	Nott, Douglas	U. of Detroit	L. Half	21	188	Ann Arbor, Mich.
37	Akerstrom, George	Colgate	Center	22	187	Whitestone, L.I.
41	Monahan, J. Regis	Ohio State	L. Guard	23	210	Pittsburgh, Pa.
43	Lund, Francis	U. of Minnesota	L. Half	21	180	Rice Lake, Wis.
48	Brooke, Lewis	Colgate	R. Tackle	22	200	Bayside, L.I.
54	Larson, Frank	U. of Minnesota	R. End	22	198	Duluth, Minn.
70	Roughton, Philip	U. of Minnesota	R. Tackle	21	208	St. Paul, Minn.
74	Pacetti, Mario	U. of Wisconsin	R. Guard	21	210	Kenosha, Wis.
88	Boganski, Joseph	Colgate	R. End	24	190	New Britain, Conn.
88	Purvis, Duane	Purdue	R. Half	21	194	Mattoon, Ill.
99	Barclay, George	U. of N.C.	R. Guard	23	184	Natrona, Pa.

✶ ALL-STAR WEST TEAM ✶
ROSTER

No.	Name	College	Position	Age	Weight	Height	Home Town
00	Berry, Roy	Tulsa U.	Half	22	157	5.7	Shawnee, Oklahoma
4	Salatino, Joe	Santa Clara	Quarter	22	167	6.0	Tacoma, Wash.
7	Fuqua, Raymond	Southern Methodist	End	22	185	6.0	Shreveport, La.
10	Sobrero, Frank	Santa Clara	Half	21	197	6.1	Oakland, Calif.
13	Warburton, Irvine	U.S.C.	Quarter	21	148	5.6	Los Angeles, Calif.
18	Clemens, Cal	U.S.C.	Half	21	197	5.11	Los Angeles, Calif.
21	Meier, Franklin	Nebraska U.	Center	21	175	6.1	Lincoln, Neb.
28	Simmering, Lawrence	U.S.F.	Center	20	210	6.2	Lodi, Calif.
30	Mucha, Chas.	Washington U.	Guard	21	198	5.10	Chicago, Ill.
31	Barber, Jas.	U.S.F.	Tackle	22	215	6.3	Manteca, Calif.
33	Hilliard, Bohn	Texas U.	Half	23	165	5.8½	Orange, Texas
35	Stacey, Jas.	Oklahoma U.	Guard	22	200	6.2½	Altus, Oklahoma
41	Stojack, Frank	Washington State	Guard	21	193	5.11½	Tacoma, Wash.
45	Hubbard, Wesley	Olympic Club	End	23	190	6.0	San Jose, Calif.
48	Theodoratos, Geo.	Washington U.	Guard	22	240	6.2	Sacramento, Calif.
50	Carter, Clyde	Southern Methodist	Tackle	23	205	6.1½	Denton, Texas
54	Maddox, Geo.	Kansas State	Tackle	23	217	6.3	Greenville, Texas
51	Nichelini, Allen	St. Mary's	Full	21	195	6.0	St. Helena, Calif.
69	Pernino, Felix	St. Mary's	End	21	190	6.0	Los Angeles, Calif.
70	Ullin, Woodrow	Washington U.	Tackle	21	193	6.1	Centralia, Wash.
75	Morse, Ray	Oregon U.	End	21	195	6.1½	Portland, Ore.
76	Sulkosky, Paul	Washington U.	Full	21	195	5.10½	Puyallup, Wash.

OFFICIAL SOUVENIR PROGRAM
All Star East
vs.
All Star West
Tenth Annual Game American Football
KEZAR STADIUM
Tuesday, January 1, 1935.
Military Pageant 2 p.m.
Kickoff 2 p.m.

Auspices of Islam, Aahmes and Ben Ali Temples, A. A. O. N. M. S.,
for the Benefit of the San Francisco Unit
Shriners' Hospital for Crippled Children

PRICE TWENTY-FIVE CENTS

J. REGIS MONAHAN
Ohio State
Left Guard

GEORGE AKERSTROM
Colgate
Center

GERALD FORD
U. of Michigan
Center

FRANK LARSON
U. of Minnesota
Right End

HARRY LEEPER
Northwestern U.
Left End

DOUGLAS NOTT
U. of Detroit
Left Half

EDWARD BROMINSKI
Columbia
Right Half

GEORGE BARCLAY
U. of N.C.
Right Guard

(partial overlapping roster, right margin)

No.		Home Town
00	Ber...	
4	Sal...	
7	Fuc...	Shreveport, La.
10	Sob...	Oakland, Calif.
13	Wa...	Angeles, Calif.
18	Cle...	Angeles, Calif.
21	Me...	Lincoln, Neb.
28	Sie...	Lodi, Calif.
30	Mu...	Chicago, Ill.
31	Bar...	Manteca, Calif.
33	Hil...	Orange, Texas
35	Sta...	...tus, Oklahoma
41	Sto...	Tacoma, Wash.
45	Hu...	San Jose, Calif.
48	The...	...ramento, Calif.
50	Car...	Denton, Texas
51	Mac...	...reenville, Texas
54	Nic...	Helena, Calif.
69	Per...	Angeles, Calif.
70	Ull...	...entralia, Wash.
75	Mo...	Portland, Ore.
76	Sul...	Puyallup, Wash.

Ford said. "At the end of my second day, Pond offered me $2,400 a year if I would join him as an assistant and also coach the freshman boxing team. I knew nothing about boxing, but I promised to take instruction at the Grand Rapids YMCA before returning that fall."

Ford had another reason to jump at Pond's offer—he wanted to enroll in Yale Law School. He asked Pond whether he could take law classes while working as a coach. Pond thought his duties with the team would take up too much of his time, but he promised to relay the request to Yale's law school deans. Looking over his grades from Michigan, the deans doubted that Ford could handle his classes in addition to his coaching responsibilities. They turned down his request, but Ford decided to take Pond's offer anyway, hoping eventually to change their minds.

Ford started work at Yale in August 1935, and soon realized Pond had been correct—coaching football was a full-time job and he had been foolish to think he could have squeezed in law school during his spare time. Yale's varsity team had a good year, winning six games and losing three. Ford spent the next summer working as a ranger at Yellowstone National Park. The next fall he returned to Yale, where he helped coach a team that won the Ivy League championship. Two of the players on that team were Robert Taft Jr. and William Proxmire, both of whom would go on to serve in the U.S. Senate.

After the season, Ford again found time on his hands. This time, instead of working at a national park, Ford returned to Ann Arbor, where he took law classes at the University of Michigan. He scored B's in two classes, then returned to Yale in the fall of 1937. Again, he asked permission to take classes while coaching football. Pond reluctantly agreed, but Ford still had to convince the law school deans. This time, they agreed to let him take two classes in the spring semester, after football season. They cautioned Ford that he would have to score well in those classes to be accepted as a full-time student.

"They were reluctant—98 of the 125 members of the freshman class had made Phi Beta Kappa as undergraduates, they pointed out—but they finally agreed to let me take two courses that spring," Ford recalled. "I earned two more B's. Satisfied that I could do the work, they withdrew their rejections and accepted me full time."

Ford worked hard and graduated as a member of the Yale Law School Class of 1941. He graduated in the top 25 percent of the class, demonstrating that he certainly was up to the challenge of Yale. Among his classmates at Yale were Cyrus Vance, a future secretary of state; Potter Stewart, a future member of the U.S. Supreme Court; and Sargent Shriver, who would marry the sister of President John F. Kennedy, head the Peace Corps, and run for vice president on the Democratic ticket in 1972.

Following graduation, Ford returned to Grand Rapids, where he started a law practice with Philip Buchen, an old friend from his days living in the Delta

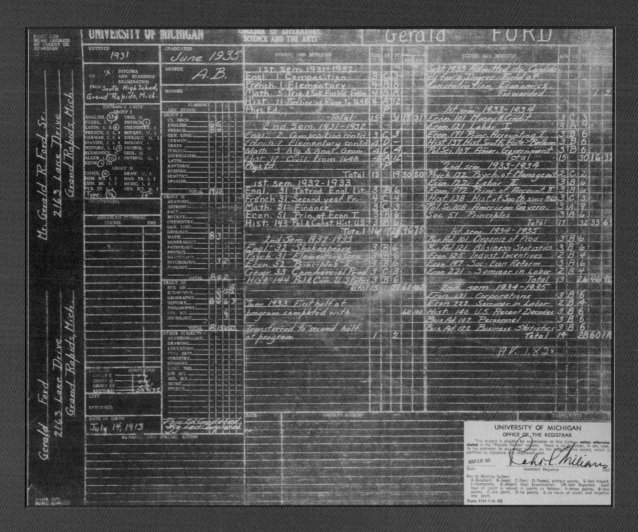

Gerald Ford's transcript from the University of Michigan, which he attended from 1931 to 1935. Ford graduated from the University of Michigan with a 1.82 grade-point average and a liberal arts degree. He received A's in four courses during his four years at the university—European History from the Decline of Rome to 1648, Western Civilization Since 1648, Labor I, and American Government.

Kappa Delta fraternity on the Michigan campus. There was little time to devote to the practice of law, though. Just a few months after Ford returned to Grand Rapids, the Japanese launched an attack on the U.S. naval base at Pearl Harbor. Ford enlisted in the U.S. Navy and saw action in the South Pacific during World War II aboard an aircraft carrier.

He returned to Grand Rapids following the war and resumed the practice of law. In 1948, he won his first election, a seat in the U.S. House of Representatives. He took a brief time off during that campaign to marry Elizabeth Bloomer, whom everyone called Betty. Jerry and Betty Ford would raise four children, Michael, John, Steven, and Susan.

A Republican, Ford remained in the House throughout the 1950s, turning down offers from GOP leaders in Michigan to run for governor and the U.S. Senate. Instead, Ford gained stature and influence in the House, and in 1963 was elected chairman of the House Republican Conference—the third most important leadership post in the GOP caucus.

Coach Gerald Ford (rear row, third from left) and the Yale University Boxing Team, 1936. When the Yale University football coach needed an assistant, he offered Ford $2,400 per year—then a fairly good salary—to work as assistant line coach, junior varsity coach, and as coach of Yale's boxing team. "Of boxing," said Ford, "I knew next to nothing. No, that's not right. I knew absolutely nothing."

Ford accepted the job, hoping to realize two dreams at once—to stay in football and to pursue a long-nurtured aspiration to attend law school. However, the admissions officer was convinced that he could not handle both law school and a full-time job. Finally, in 1938, Ford obtained permission to take two courses on a trial basis. He did sufficiently well to be allowed to increase to a full-time program the following semester. "I was warned that of the 125 law students entering that year," said Ford, "ninety-eight were Phi Beta Kappa, and that was clearly another league from the one I had been in. Somehow, I got by."

After the assassination of President Kennedy in November 1963, Ford was appointed to the Warren Commission, which investigated the assassination and concluded that there had been no conspiracy to kill the president, and that gunman Lee Harvey Oswald had acted alone. Over the years, skeptics have criticized the conclusion and the evidence on which the commission relied, but no one has ever been able to offer convincing proof of a conspiracy to kill the president.

In 1965, with Democrats in control of Congress, Ford was elected House Minority Leader, the top GOP leadership post in the House.

In 1972, while President Richard M. Nixon was on his way to scoring a landslide victory in his reelection campaign, reports surfaced that a group of burglars employed by the president's campaign committee had been arrested with electronic eavesdropping equipment during a break-in at the Democratic National Committee office in the Watergate office complex in Washington.

The scandal that grew out of the break-in became known as Watergate. In late 1973, a separate scandal engulfed Vice President Spiro T. Agnew, forcing him to resign amid charges that he evaded income taxes. When Agnew resigned, Nixon selected Ford to serve as the new vice president.

In August of 1974, the Watergate scandal finally caught up with Nixon. He became the first president to resign from office, and Ford was sworn in to take his place. As such, Ford became the only president in history to have been appointed to the job under the terms of presidential succession spelled out in the U.S. Constitution.

For Ford, it would be a brief stay in the White House. Soon after taking office, he decided to issue a presidential pardon for Nixon, preventing prosecutors from seeking indictments against the former president. That decision haunted him as the 1976 election approached. During the race that fall against Democrat Jimmy Carter, Ford committed a major blunder when he declared during a televised debate that "there is no Soviet domination of Eastern Europe, and there never will be under a Ford administration."

The former Soviet Union had, of course, dominated many of the Eastern European countries since the closing days of World War II, sponsoring puppet regimes in Poland, Romania, East Germany, and other countries, and marching troops into Czechoslovakia to stifle rebellions. Ford tried to clarify his remarks following the debate, but Americans found themselves doubting his competency as president and Carter won the election of 1976.

After taking the oath of office and being sworn in as the nation's thirty-ninth president, Jimmy Carter's first words were, "For myself and for our nation, I want to thank my predecessor for all he has done to heal our land."

—Hal Marcovitz

Jimmy Carter
Chapter Thirty-eight

From the time he was a boy, Jimmy Carter wanted to become a naval officer. Growing up in a rural Georgia town named Plains, Jimmy had never seen the ocean, much less the huge U.S. Navy battleships and destroyers he hoped one day to command. His interest was piqued by his Uncle Tom Gordy, who had joined the Navy as an enlisted man and was, as the recruiting posters promised, seeing the world. Every few weeks, young Jimmy would receive a picture postcard from Uncle Tom announcing his latest port of call. Soon, Jimmy had a collection of postcards from Marseille, Gibraltar, Amsterdam, Athens, the Panama Canal, Pearl Harbor, Manila, Hong Kong, Pago Pago, and Sydney, among other places. Occasionally, Uncle Tom would send a gift—a model sampan, for example, or a tiny enameled box with oriental dragons painted on it. Jimmy treasured these gifts, for they had planted the hope that he would be a Navy man, too.

On June 30, 1943, with the Second World War raging in Europe and the South Pacific, eighteen-year-old Jimmy Carter took a major step toward fulfilling his dream when he stepped onto the campus of the U.S. Naval Academy in Annapolis, Maryland. He was sworn in as a "plebe"—a freshman student soon to face three years of vigorous training, testing, and physical endurance. Jimmy had studied hard and prepared himself for years for this opportunity, and he resolved that no task at Annapolis would cause him to fail in his goal of graduating as an officer of the U.S. Navy.

However, Jimmy had not counted on the rituals of hazing at the academy. For decades, hazing was a common practice on many college campuses, but no place was it practiced with such relish and cruelty as on the campuses of America's military academies—Annapolis and West Point, where future officers of the U.S. Army are trained. Plebes at both schools found themselves at the beck and call of upperclassmen, who could force them to perform ridiculous and demeaning chores simply to provide amusement for other students. Sometimes, the plebes at Annapolis were woken up early and forced to run through the campus obstacle course chased by sadistic upperclassmen. Plebes were told to row heavy boats

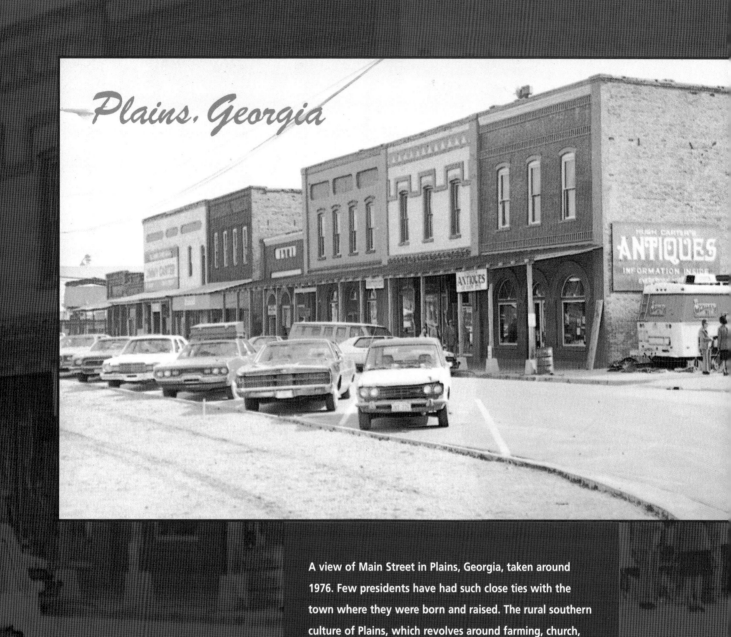

Plains, Georgia

A view of Main Street in Plains, Georgia, taken around 1976. Few presidents have had such close ties with the town where they were born and raised. The rural southern culture of Plains, which revolves around farming, church, and school, had an enormous influence on molding the character and shaping the political policies of the thirty-ninth president of the United States.

The Plains High School basketball team, 1940. Jimmy Carter is in the back row, second from left (number ten).

In his *Memoirs* and in many interviews and speeches, Carter has stated that the principal influences on his education were his hometown of Plains, Georgia; the Plains High School; the Plains Baptist Church; and his studies at the United States Naval Academy at Annapolis, Maryland.

against the current across the Severn River, which flowed through the campus. Other times, plebes were told to snap to attention and recite inane poems or sing songs. Jimmy endured the hardships of hazing, knowing it was part of the Annapolis experience. He forced himself to do whatever the upperclassmen commanded, until the day a senior told him to stand at attention and sing the Civil War song "Marching Through Georgia." Jimmy flatly refused.

The song, written by Henry Clay Work in 1865, celebrates the victory of the Union Army under General William Tecumseh Sherman, whose "March to the Sea" helped destroy the Confederacy. Sherman led his men on a cruel rampage through Georgia and other states, burning farms and looting homes as they swept aside rebel resistance. Before their march was over Sherman's men destroyed Georgia's capital, Atlanta.

Jimmy Carter did not have much interest in the history of the Civil War, but because he grew up in the South, he had come to respect the rebel cause and the sacrifices his ancestors had made for a fight they believed was just. To Southern whites, "Marching Through Georgia" was regarded as an insult. The song contains these lyrics:

Sherman's dashing Yankee boys will never make the coast!
So the saucy rebels said 'twas a handsome boast
Had they not forgot, alas! To reckon with the Host
While we were marching through Georgia.

Plebes who refused an upperclassman's orders found themselves subjected to severe punishments. They were told to bend over and grab their toes so their rumps could be paddled with wooden soup spoons or planks of wood. In the dining hall, they were forced to eat their meals while sitting under their tables. Or, they may have been ordered to assume a sitting posture at the table, but instructed not to let their posteriors touch their chairs. After a few minutes, the pain of stooping while eating could become unbearable. Jimmy endured the punishments, but for the remainder of his year as a plebe he steadfastly refused to sing "Marching Through Georgia."

Years later, as Carter was campaigning for the presidency of the United States, he visited Phoenix, Arizona. To welcome him, a high school marching band played "Marching Through Georgia." Jimmy Carter, whose warm and wide smile had captivated voters, suddenly grew sullen. "Doesn't anybody realize that's not a southern song?" he asked.

James Earl Carter Jr. was born October 1, 1924, in Plains Hospital. He was the first U.S. president born in a hospital. His father was James Earl Carter Sr., a prosperous but by no means wealthy farmer and storekeeper whom everyone called Earl. His mother, Lillian Gordy Carter, had been educated as a nurse. In keeping with southern custom, she was called Miss Lillian. Jimmy was the oldest of the Carters' four children.

For Jimmy, childhood was a Huck Finn existence. He rarely wore shoes or a shirt in the spring and summer. He fished for eels and catfish in the Kinchafoonee Creek. He climbed trees and went hunting for possums and raccoons with his father. His playmates were mostly the African-American children of the poor farm workers who lived in shacks on his father's land. Jimmy would have few white friends until he enrolled in the Plains school. Like every Southern town during the 1920s, Plains was segregated. That meant white children went to one school while black children went to another.

Jimmy entered Plains School in September 1930, one month before his sixth birthday. The school was relatively new. It had been erected just nine years before. First through eleventh grades were taught in the same building. The elementary school was housed in the east wing while high school students took classes in the north and west wings.

Jimmy was one of the brightest children in the elementary school wing, a fact attributed mostly to the influence of Miss Lillian. She was a voracious reader who passed her love for books on to her children, particularly Jimmy. When he was five years old, Jimmy's godmother sent him the complete works of the French writer Guy de Maupassant. Jimmy was too young to read the stories then, but he would eventually read them all. In the third grade, Jimmy received a prize for reading the most books. The reward for the contest was lunch at the teacher's house.

Many of the students at the school in Plains went on to college, which was a remarkable achievement for children of the rural South during the Great Depression. Carter—and nearly everyone else who went to school in Plains from the 1920s to the 1950s—attributed the school's success to one woman, Julia Coleman. "I have never known of a teacher who had such a profound impact on students as she did," Carter said years later.

Miss Julia, as she was known around school, inspired her students to see beyond the tiny world of Plains and the rural South. She urged them to read, of course, but not just schoolbooks. Miss Julia's students read poetry and developed an interest in art and music. She engaged them in conversations about national and international events and forced them to become debaters. She had a particular talent for recognizing intelligence in her students and challenging them to make the most of their abilities.

Jimmy spent his eighth-grade year in Miss Julia's classroom. At the conclusion of the year, Miss Julia recommended that Jimmy read *War and Peace* over the summer. The 1,400-page novel about Napoleon's invasion of Russia is not an easy read for most adults; for a thirteen-year-old boy it might have proven to be an overwhelming task. But Jimmy resolved to read the book, thinking at first it was a Western adventure featuring gun-toting cowboys and Indians on the warpath. Of course, *War and Peace* has nothing to do with cowboys and Indians. Written between 1863 and 1869 by Russian author Leo Tolstoy, the novel is complicated, featuring more than five hundred characters whose lives are affected by the war between Russia and France early in the nineteenth century. The overwhelming theme of the book is that war is evil, and while princes and army generals may find fame and valor in the fighting, it is ordinary people who suffer the most. Jimmy finished the book that summer and, in fact, would read Tolstoy's masterpiece again two more times by the time he was an adult. No book would have more of an effect on his outlook during his four years as president, or in the years that followed, during which he served his country as an internationally known diplomat. The message of *War and Peace*, Carter said later, was "to show that the course of human events— even great historical events—is determined ultimately not by the leaders, but by the common ordinary people. Their hopes and dreams, their doubts and fears, their courage and tenacity, their quiet commitment to determine the destiny of the world."

Despite his love for reading, Jimmy was hardly what anyone would call "bookish." He was athletic and competed on the basketball and track teams. He joined the Future Farmers of America. He took up woodworking, an avocation that would become a lifelong passion. He dated girls, worked in his father's store, and went hunting and fishing.

"The course of human events…is determined ultimately not by the leaders, but by the common ordinary people. Their hopes and dreams, their doubts and fears, their courage and tenacity, their quiet commitment to determine the destiny of the world."

Carter is in the front row, right side (squatting down) in this photograph of the Plains High School class of 1941.

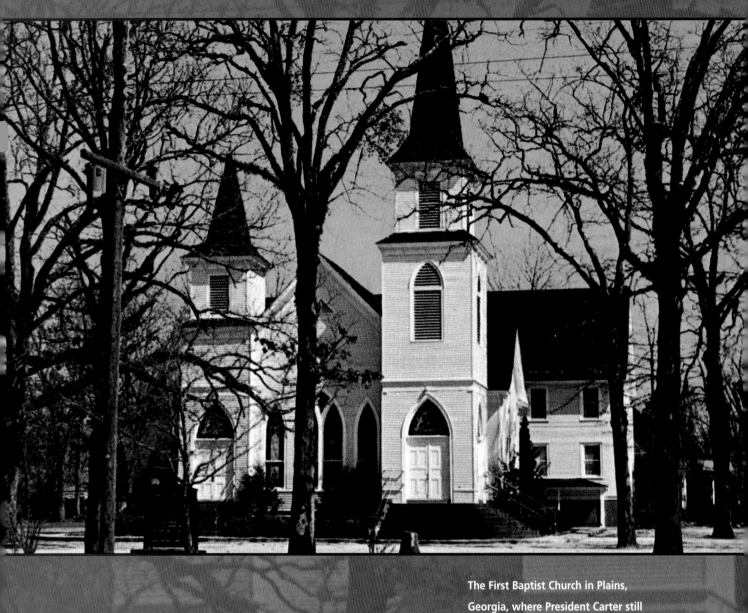

The First Baptist Church in Plains, Georgia, where President Carter still teaches a Sunday school class. (This photo was taken around 1976.) The church website states, "This unique situation gives us an opportunity to share with many people who have never before had any close exposure to the Gospel message. This opportunity also represents a responsibility which we take very seriously."

He also maintained his fascination with the Navy. While still in elementary school, Jimmy wrote to Annapolis asking for the school's catalog without, of course, revealing his age. The catalog became a much-cherished possession and Jimmy read and re-read it many times, memorizing the criteria he would have to meet in order to be accepted as a midshipman. "It was the driving force in my life," he said later.

Some parts of the catalog puzzled him, though. For example, he fretted for years that his toothy smile would cause him to be turned down. The catalog warned that candidates who suffered an overbite—referred to in the catalog as a "malocclusion of the teeth"—would not be considered.

The malocclusion turned out to be a trivial issue that would have no effect on his application to Annapolis. His grades would not stand in his way, either. As he approached graduation, Jimmy's grades were among the best at Plains High School; he would have been valedictorian had it not been for an ill-advised prank. Jimmy and some friends played hooky just a few weeks before graduation. They were caught and punished. In Jimmy's case, the punishment included denial of valedictory honors. Still, when Jimmy graduated from Plains High School on June 2, 1941, he was one of three commencement speakers.

Nevertheless, the one handicap that Jimmy could not overcome was the lack of political influence required to obtain an appointment to Annapolis. Backing by the local member of Congress was necessary to obtain admission to the service academies. In Sumter County, the congressman was Democrat Stephen Pace. Earl Carter knew his son's ambitions, and he knew it would take Pace's help to win Jimmy an appointment to Annapolis. By 1938, Earl Carter was an influential farmer and businessman in Sumter County. He contributed money to Pace's congressional campaign that year as well as in 1940 and helped campaign for him in Plains. However, when Jimmy graduated from Plains High School Pace decided to secure an appointment to Annapolis for another boy.

Pace promised to reconsider Jimmy in 1942. In the meantime, he recommended to Earl and Lillian that they send their boy to Georgia Southwestern College, a tiny two-year school located in the nearby town of Americus. The school was small, consisting of just some two hundred students. It included just one classroom building, two dormitories, and a gymnasium. Tuition was $204 a year, which Earl paid.

Georgia Southwestern was not Annapolis, but Jimmy made the most of his time at the school. He knew he needed to keep his grades up, so he studied hard. He also joined the basketball team and got involved in student activities. He joined a fraternity and was elected vice president of the freshman class. During his first semester at Georgia Southwestern he lived at home and took a bus to Americus for classes. He moved into a dormitory for his second semester. His baby brother Billy had been born that year and Jimmy felt crowded at home, sharing the modest Carter family house in Plains with his parents, two sisters, and a baby.

Congressman Pace made good on his promise to Earl and won an appointment for Jimmy to Annapolis in 1942. By then, the Japanese had attacked Pearl Harbor, drawing the United States into World War II. It is likely that if Jimmy hadn't been appointed to the academy, he would have been drafted and sent off to combat as an enlisted man. Still, he would have to wait yet another year before enrolling at Annapolis. Jimmy lacked a background in the science and engineering courses he would need as a midshipman. The Navy recommended that he spend a year at Georgia Institute of Technology in Atlanta, where he could study science and also take courses in navigation and seamanship as a member of the Reserve Officers' Training Corps. Jimmy agreed, and enrolled that fall at Georgia Tech.

Jimmy hated city life. He joined few college organizations and rarely spent a weekend on the Atlanta campus, preferring instead to take the bus home to Plains. He studied hard, though, and at the end of his year at Georgia Tech placed in the top 10 percent of his class and made honor roll.

Finally, in the summer of 1943, he started classes at Annapolis. Ordinarily, the service academies require four years to obtain a degree, but during World War II the Army and Navy were both in need of young officers so the courses were accelerated so that they could be completed in three years.

Carter and the other midshipmen rose at 6:15 A.M. every morning and spent their entire day in class or field training of some sort. They had little time to themselves, and even their weekends were dominated by their studies. Jimmy endured it all—the study, physical tests, discipline, and even the hazing. "He would never let it out," said Arthur Middletown, one of his classmates at Annapolis, "never kick a chair or throw a book like the rest of us."

Slowly, Carter inched his way toward graduation. Each summer, the midshipmen were assigned to duty aboard warships. In the summer of 1944, Carter saw duty aboard the U.S.S. *New York*, an old battleship that patrolled the North Atlantic. Mostly, the *New York* seemed to spend the war dodging torpedoes launched from German U-boats. During Carter's summer aboard the *New York*, a U-boat torpedo clipped the ship's propeller. The *New York* made for port for repairs, but the damaged propeller caused the ship to lurch violently all the way home. It was an exciting summer. Carter held a variety of jobs aboard the *New York*. His favorite job was manning a forty-millimeter antiaircraft gun during alerts. His least favorite job was cleaning toilets that had a habit of overflowing on the old ship.

During Carter's second summer as a midshipman, he was called on deck along with the rest of the crew to hear a radio transmission broadcast by President Harry Truman. While standing at attention on deck, Carter heard the president announce that an atomic bomb had just been dropped on the Japanese city of Hiroshima. World War II was over. Jimmy Carter would not, at least in the foreseeable future, be serving as an officer aboard a navy ship during a time of war.

Jimmy Carter graduated from Annapolis in June 1946 and was commissioned an ensign in the U.S. Navy. A few days later he married Eleanor

DRESS PARADE, U. S. NAVAL ACADEMY, ANNAPOLIS, MD.

PICKERING PHOTO

1A3129

Looking Across Smoke Park, showing Seaward Terrace of Bancroft Hall.

22

U. S. Naval Academy, Annapolis, Md.

60666

Midshipmen Preparing for Sailboat Drill, U. S. Naval Academy, Annapolis, Md.

OFFICIAL U. S. NAVY PHOTOGRAPH

1B-H2267

Colored postcards show scenes at Annapolis, circa 1941–45.

The United States Naval Academy at Annapolis, Maryland, was established in 1845 as an undergraduate college to prepare young people to be effective naval and marine officers. The four-year course of study is similar to that of leading technical colleges except that in addition to scientific and cultural studies, there are specialized courses relating to the sea and to the profession of the naval officer.

Jimmy Carter graduated from the Naval Academy in 1946 with the accelerated class of 1947.

Rosalynn Smith in a small ceremony in Plains. Rosalynn was a friend of Jimmy's sister Ruth; she had started dating Jimmy a year earlier. The Carters would raise a family of three sons and a daughter.

Carter's Navy career would eventually lead him into service under Admiral Hyman Rickover, who spearheaded the Navy's efforts to develop nuclear submarines. During the program, though, Carter was forced to resign his commission when his father died and Miss Lillian asked him to return to Plains to take over the family farm and business. He reluctantly agreed, and on October 9, 1953, Jimmy Carter left the U.S. Navy and the career he had dreamed about since first receiving his Uncle Tom's postcards as a boy.

Carter entered politics in 1962, winning a disputed election to a seat in the Georgia State Senate. Initially, it appeared that Carter had lost the election, but he was able to prove that his opponent's victory was based on widespread voting fraud. He appealed, and a judge threw out votes cast by people either dead or in prison. The subsequent recount showed Carter the winner. In 1966, he lost the Democratic primary for governor of Georgia, but ran for the position again in 1970 and won. He became one of the first southern politicians to support racial integration. *Time* magazine featured him on its cover in 1971, and both the *Washington Post* and *Life* magazine declared Carter a representative of the "New South."

In 1972, Carter sought to win his party's vice presidential nomination at the Democratic National Convention. His campaign fell short and Carter was left off the ticket. He resolved to make another run for a national ticket in 1976, this time as his party's presidential nominee. When the 1976 campaign began, Carter was a little-known former governor of a southern state, and political experts gave him little chance of winning the Democratic nomination in a field that featured such heavyweight contenders as Congressman Morris Udall and Senators Henry Jackson and Birch Bayh. But the public seemed to connect with his down-home ways and Southern charm, and Carter scored impressive victories in the early primaries and was soon viewed as the front-runner. That fall, he defeated the incumbent president, Gerald R. Ford, who found himself weighed down by his pardon of President Richard M. Nixon following Nixon's resignation from the White House in the aftermath of the Watergate scandal.

As president, Carter became a defender of international human rights. In September 1978 he hosted a historic summit to encourage peace talks between Egypt and Israel. At home, though, his efforts resulted in far fewer successes. He was unable to rescue the economy from a deep recession. Meanwhile, America's stature as a world power suffered during Carter's presidency. In 1979, militant Islamic students in Iran seized the U.S. embassy and held members of the diplomatic staff hostage for fourteen months. When a military rescue attempt failed in the Iranian desert, Carter took the blame. Ultimately, he was unable to negotiate the release of the hostages before the election of 1980, and he lost to Republican Ronald Reagan.

Carter has spent his post-presidential years as an active member of the world community. He has traveled from country to country, crisis to crisis, using his talents as a negotiator to help broker cease-fires, bring relief to famine-stricken areas, and ensure free elections. He also became an active volunteer for Habitat for Humanity, helping to build homes for the needy in the United States and abroad. In 2002, he was awarded the Nobel Peace Prize.

During his acceptance speech in Oslo, Norway, Jimmy Carter talked about the influences on his life. He mentioned Julia Coleman, saying, "When I was a young boy, this teacher introduced me to Leo Tolstoy's novel *War and Peace*. She interpreted that powerful narrative as a reminder that the simple human attributes of goodness and truth can overcome great power. She also taught us that an individual is not swept along a tide of inevitability but can influence even the greatest human events."

—Hal Marcovitz

Ronald Reagan
Chapter Thirty-nine

When Ronald Reagan arrived at tiny Eureka College in Illinois in the fall of 1928, he found what he thought was a sleepy campus composed of aging ivy-covered classroom buildings and dormitories, streets lined with shady elm trees, and a creaky old football stadium that came alive on Saturday afternoons. At Eureka, the young man who would become the fortieth president of the United States found a way to escape the hard times his family knew in nearby Dixon.

Eureka College, however, was on the verge of rebellion in the fall of 1928. Students and faculty members were quite vocal about demanding changes in the way college president Bert Wilson and the board of trustees had run the school for decades. Eureka's administrators complied with strict rules set down by the school's sponsor, the Disciples of Christ Church. Daily chapel attendance was mandatory, and dancing at campus events was prohibited. Even students caught attending dances at such harmless off-campus affairs as American Legion–sponsored mixers were severely punished. Women had to adhere to a strict dress code that required skirts to be worn down to their calves.

The students wanted the rules to be eased. For the most part, faculty members were sympathetic to the students' complaints. The faculty had its own complaints about President Wilson. They believed the curriculum was outdated. They felt the college, a shoestring operation to begin with, was nevertheless suffering because of Wilson's parsimonious attitude and his willingness to cut budgets. When Wilson proposed combining several departments, laying off six professors and cutting the salaries of others, what had long been a quiet contrariness by teachers about Wilson's administration suddenly became a very public show of rancor.

The students wanted Wilson to resign. Student leaders proposed a strike—they wanted all students to stay out of classes until Wilson stepped down. Late in the fall, the students met in the school chapel to debate the issue. Although the upperclassmen were leading the revolt, they felt a freshman should propose the strike. The upperclassmen were too close to graduation and feared that if the ploy failed, they would be dismissed from school and denied their diplomas.

...we wore knee pants and black stockings and when our shoes wore out we put cardboard in the bottoms...

Ronald Reagan, age eight, is in the second row at far left with his hand on chin in this 1919 photograph of his third-grade class at Tampico Grade School, Illinois. Nellie Darby, his teacher, is at upper right. Reagan's best grade school chum Denison (whom Dutch called Newt) later told an interviewer that they "attended all the silent Westerns, gaining free admission by carrying coal to the Opera House where they were shown." Denison recalled:

[On Sundays] we wore knee pants and black stockings and when our shoes wore out we put cardboard in the bottoms and when we got holes in our stockings we painted in shoe polish to cover 'em up. We stole a few grapes and some apples. . . .We had this janitor at the school. In the fall we'd all come down and help him rake up the leaves and we'd stay for a big marshmallow roast. We didn't play ball on Sunday. . . . We had to go to church and then have the family dinner and not much rough play.

In 1920, the Reagan family settled in Dixon, Illinois, a small town of nearly 8,200 residents about a hundred miles west of Chicago. The Reagans lived in a modest rented three-bedroom house—their fifth new town and seventh house in the previous nine years. Dutch, now nine years old, remembered his childhood in Dixon as the happiest period of his life. "We didn't know we were poor because the people around us were of the same circumstance," wrote the future president. Dixon was Ronald Reagan's first permanent home. "All of us have a place to go back to. Dixon is that place for me," he later wrote. "There was the life that shaped my mind and my body for all the years to come after."

Reagan was enrolled in the fifth grade at South Central Grammar School, a five-minute walk from his home. He then attended South Dixon High School, transferring to North Dixon in his sophomore year.

During his junior year at North Dixon High School, 1926–27, Reagan played guard for the varsity football team. The caption for this photograph in the 1927 school yearbook, *The Dixonian*, read, "'Dutch,' the lightest but fastest guard on the team, won his letter through sheer grit. With 'Dutch' returning to the squad, things look good for Dixon in 1927." Reagan excelled in athletics and he also had strong interests in dramatics, creative writing, drawing, and school politics.

The freshman selected to stand before the student body and propose the strike was Ronald Reagan. He was a popular member of the freshman class, a leader among his fellow students and, as a member of the drama club, somebody who appeared at ease in front of an audience. Although hardly a student radical, Reagan accepted the challenge.

"I'd been told that I should sell the idea so there'd be no doubt of the outcome," Reagan recalled. "I discovered that night that an audience had a feel to it and in the parlance of the theater, that audience and I were together. When I came to actually presenting the motion there was no need for parliamentary procedure; they came to their feet with a roar—even the faculty members present voted by acclamation. It was heady wine."

For Reagan, this would be one of his first opportunities to use his natural powers as a communicator to persuade an audience of his position—it was even reported that one of the female students in attendance that evening fainted under the spell of his rhetoric.

The student strike commenced the day after Thanksgiving break. For the next week, only eight of the school's two hundred and twenty students attended classes (two of the students were President Wilson's daughters). Reporters swarmed to the tiny Eureka campus to report the news about the student uprising. On December 7, 1928, President Wilson submitted his resignation to the board of trustees and the students returned to classes.

Years later, when Reagan was governor of California, he encountered a similar student uprising at the University of California at Berkeley over a series of cuts in the university's budget proposed by the state government. As governor, Reagan was far less sympathetic to the plight of the Berkeley students and faculty members who supported them than he had been as a leader of the Eureka campus uprising. "It is disturbing to see supposedly mature members of the academic community inciting students to intemperate acts with inflammatory charges," he huffed at the time.

Of course, by then, Ronald Reagan had received a thorough schooling in the conservative ideology that would come to dominate his political career and eventually his presidency.

Ronald Wilson Reagan was born February 6, 1911, in Tampico, Illinois, a small town about ninety miles west of Chicago. He was the second son of Jack and Nelle Reagan. His mother was a devoted churchgoer, his father a shoe salesman and hopeless alcoholic.

Although the Reagans were of Scotch-Irish ancestry, the little boy was called "Dutch" almost from the moment of his birth. Upon seeing his second son in the hospital, Jack called him a "fat little Dutchman."

There is no question the Reagans were a close family, but life was a struggle for them. Jack Reagan's jobs in the shoe business were invariably low-paying; his drinking put a further strain on the family. By the time Dutch entered the first grade at Filas Willard School in February 1916 in Galesburg, a town near the Iowa border, the Reagans had already been forced to move three times.

Still, Nelle Reagan brought warmth to the home. Dutch and his older brother Neil loved snuggling close to their mother while she read to them. They particularly loved adventure stories, such as the exploits of the Three Musketeers or King Arthur and the Knights of the Round Table.

Dutch could read before he entered the first grade. Nelle Reagan taught her son to read in the parlor of their Galesburg home by having him follow her fingers as she pointed to words on the page. "One evening," Reagan later recalled, "all the funny black marks on the paper clicked into place."

The fact that little Dutch could read at age five was a source of pride among the Reagans. Nelle would often invite neighbors in to listen to her boy read articles from the Galesburg newspaper.

During Dutch's second year at Filas Willard, Jack Reagan's drinking cost him his job and the family was forced to move again, this time to nearby Monmouth, Illinois. Jack found a job selling shoes in the E.B. Colwell Department Store, and Dutch and Neil enrolled in Monmouth Central School.

Dutch did not adjust easily to school in Monmouth. He was nearsighted and had trouble reading the blackboard, but his parents were unaware of his problem and no effort was made to correct his vision. He also made few friends in Monmouth; evidently, his classmates were jealous of him. "He was startling to look at, not only good-looking but he had this air about him," recalled a Monmouth classmate, Gertrude Crockett. "I used to turn around in class just to stare back at him. His jaw was always set—as though somebody was going to take a poke at him and he was ready for the punches... I looked at his thrust-out chin every day and wondered, 'Why?'"

Other classmates were much more cruel. Dutch would often be chased home from school by bullies; later, when he returned to Monmouth to campaign for the presidency, he told local citizens that his mad dashes home were the only times in his life when he had been truly terrified.

In the summer of 1919 the Reagans moved again, this time back to Tampico, where Jack had the opportunity to manage a shoe store. Dutch entered the third grade that fall at Tampico Grade School. He wasn't much for studying, but he was generally an "A" student because he discovered he had a photographic memory. Dutch's favorite subject was American history; he could easily recall the dates of battles and scored well on tests.

It was at this time that Dutch developed a love for football—a sport he much preferred over baseball because his poor eyesight made it hard for him to hit the ball. Each day, he would hurry home from school for the sandlot games his friends played in his Tampico neighborhood. "We chose up sides, backed up to the limits of the field, and one of us kicked off," he recalled. "Then, screaming and waving our arms we descended on the unlucky kid who caught it. Everyone piled on top of him."

In December 1920 the Reagans moved once again. Jack had become part owner of the Fashion Boot Shop, a shoe store in Dixon, a small town about seventy-five miles west of Chicago. Jack Reagan's finances would improve little in Dixon, however. Although he managed the store, he was in debt to his partner and brought home little money over the next few years. Nevertheless, this was the last time the Reagan family had to move. Dixon became Dutch's permanent home until he left for college.

Located along the Rock River, Dixon was then a town of some ten thousand people. All the streets were lined with trees. On the main street, Galena Avenue, a visitor might stay at the town's largest hotel, the Nachusa House, where Abraham Lincoln spent a night in 1856 when he arrived in town to debate Stephen A. Douglas. Dixon's South Central Grammar School, where Dutch enrolled, was a red brick building erected during the Civil War. The Reagans rented a house on South Hennepin Avenue. The rent was $23 a month, which Jack Reagan was hard-pressed to meet. The family did find the money for eyeglasses for Dutch, though; by then, his eye problems had been diagnosed.

During their summers in Dixon, Nelle started taking Dutch to the Chautauqua shows held on campgrounds outside of town. Often staged beneath large tents, the Chautauqua shows included Bible readings and other religious lectures, but there were also theatrical productions. This was probably Dutch's first exposure to any sort of live theater. Neil, the more rebellious of the two Reagan

In April 1927, the North Dixon High School junior class presented Philip Barry's play *You and I*. (In 1923, *You and I*, a comedy about life and manners among the socially privileged, had been performed one hundred and seventy times on the Broadway stage.) Reagan and Margaret "Mugs" Cleaver, his high school girlfriend, received top billing playing sweethearts. They are shown sitting on the sofa in the top picture. Dutch is kneeling and playing the banjo in the bottom photograph (detail to the right).

children, did all he could to stay away from the Chautauqua shows, but Dutch was an enthusiastic member of the audiences.

In the summer of 1925, now a tall, muscular lad of fourteen, Dutch found work on a construction crew building the foundation for a Catholic church in Dixon. Dutch's job was to swing a pick. He spent all summer working for the crew and earned the princely sum of $200. Certainly, the impoverished Reagans could have used that money, but Nelle insisted that Dutch put the cash away for college. She was determined to see her children go to college even though most boys in Dixon dropped out of school in the eighth grade to take jobs in the local factories.

After a year at South Dixon High School, Dutch transferred to North Dixon High. There he was a member of the football team, though he sat on the bench most of his sophomore season. He was an excellent swimmer, though, and in the summer of 1926 found a job as a lifeguard in Dixon's Lowell Park. He earned $18 a week for a job he worked at seven days a week, usually twelve hours a day. He gave swimming lessons to young children, delivered the raw hamburger to the lunch stand in the mornings, showed off by performing swan dives off the diving platform, and of course made sure nobody drowned. In seven summers at Lowell Park, he was credited with saving seventy-seven lives.

At North Dixon High, Dutch befriended a young English teacher named B. J. Fraser who convinced him to join the drama club, which Fraser coached. The fact that Margaret Cleaver was also a member probably had a lot to do with Dutch's decision to join. The daughter of a local minister and the prettiest girl in Dixon,

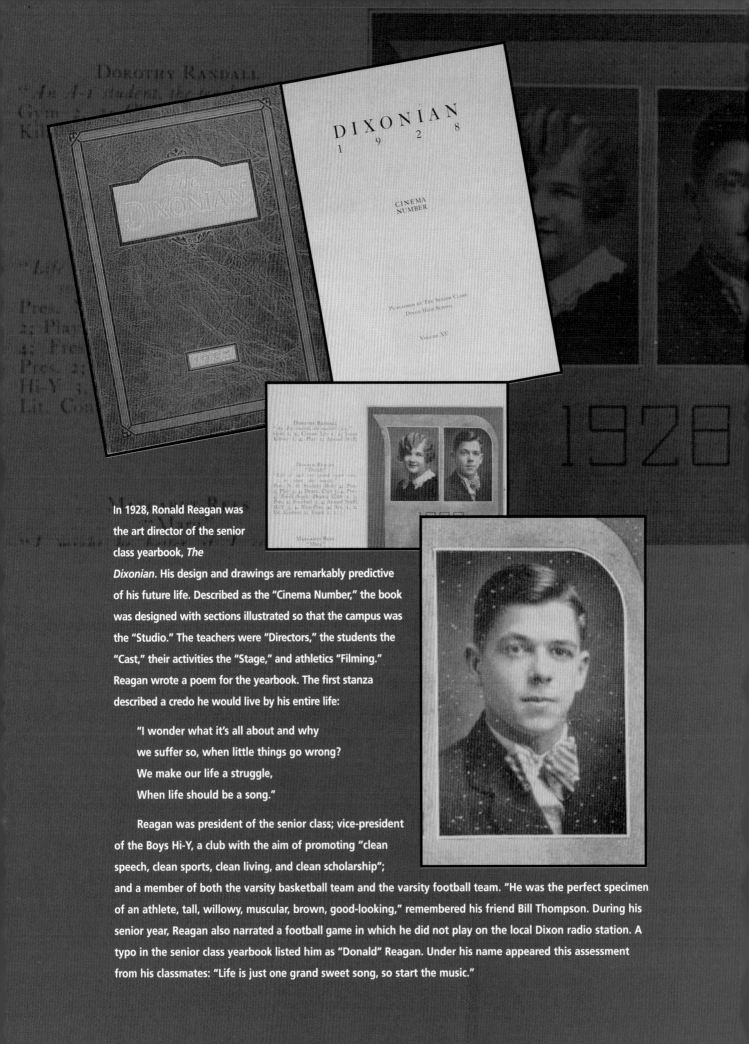

In 1928, Ronald Reagan was the art director of the senior class yearbook, *The Dixonian*. His design and drawings are remarkably predictive of his future life. Described as the "Cinema Number," the book was designed with sections illustrated so that the campus was the "Studio." The teachers were "Directors," the students the "Cast," their activities the "Stage," and athletics "Filming." Reagan wrote a poem for the yearbook. The first stanza described a credo he would live by his entire life:

> "I wonder what it's all about and why
> we suffer so, when little things go wrong?
> We make our life a struggle,
> When life should be a song."

Reagan was president of the senior class; vice-president of the Boys Hi-Y, a club with the aim of promoting "clean speech, clean sports, clean living, and clean scholarship"; and a member of both the varsity basketball team and the varsity football team. "He was the perfect specimen of an athlete, tall, willowy, muscular, brown, good-looking," remembered his friend Bill Thompson. During his senior year, Reagan also narrated a football game in which he did not play on the local Dixon radio station. A typo in the senior class yearbook listed him as "Donald" Reagan. Under his name appeared this assessment from his classmates: "Life is just one grand sweet song, so start the music."

Margaret was Dutch's steady girlfriend for most of his high school years. In his senior year, Dutch was president of the drama club. Until then, the club performed plays only for audiences composed of North Dixon students; Dutch convinced Fraser to open the plays to the public.

"He possessed a sense of presence on the stage, a sense of reality," Fraser recalled of his best student. "He fit into almost any kind of role you put him into. Wisecracking, hat-over-the-ear, cigarette-in-the-mouth reporter—he could do that as well as any sentimental scenes."

Dutch was more than just a performing artist. He submitted sketches, short stories, and poetry to the school yearbook, and several examples of his work were published.

In the classroom Dutch was a good student but hardly a scholar. He scored good grades, but relied more on his photographic memory to pass tests than on any devotion to study. On the football field, he had become a tough, gritty player unafraid of physical contact. His coach played him on the line because he wasn't fast enough to carry the ball.

As his graduation from North Dixon High approached, Dutch had his sights firmly set on attending Eureka College. Garland Waggoner, a former North Dixon football star, had gone to Eureka on a football scholarship and Dutch was anxious to follow in Waggoner's footsteps. Margaret Cleaver was also heading for Eureka. For a time, however, the school seemed out of reach. Even though he had saved about $400 from his summer jobs, Dutch lacked the resources to pay the tuition at Eureka.

In September 1928, he accompanied Margaret to Eureka and met with Dean Samuel Harrod. He asked Harrod for a football scholarship. Harrod sent him to see the football coach, Ralph "Mac" McKinzie. The coach thought Reagan was too scrawny for the team but liked his enthusiasm and told school administrators to grant Dutch an athletic scholarship that would pay for half his education. Even with the financial aid, a year of school at Eureka cost Reagan $365.

To help make ends meet, Reagan washed dishes in the Tau Kappa Epsilon fraternity house, where he lived, and also found a job busing tables in the dining room of the girls' dormitory. He majored in economics, but the classroom was not his favorite place on campus. He carried a "C" average throughout his college years. He much preferred drama club rehearsals—where he often had the lead male role— or working for the student newspaper, or football practice, even though he was far from a star on the Golden Tornadoes.

"He was nearsighted you know; couldn't see worth a damn," Coach McKinzie recalled. "Ended up at the bottom of the heap every time and missed the play because he couldn't see the man or the ball moving on him….He was very skinny at the time, and not quite as fast as the other fellows….He was a plugger, but Eureka wasn't in a position to gamble because we were not a top team even in the local area. I kept him off the field so that the other young men who were a little more aggressive playing football could carry the ball."

And yet, for years after his matriculation at Eureka Reagan would recall with fondness his experiences on the team and the guidance in life he received from McKinzie. In 1982, he returned to Eureka as president to give a speech on the fiftieth anniversary of his graduation from the school. He told this story to the students:

> I know what it's like most of the time to play up-field. One day, a bunch of us on campus decided that we ought to have a better field. The townspeople joined in and better equipment was provided, and the field was better graded. The up-hill part was in those days there were 250 of us here; in those days we were playing against schools that were 10 times your size. One day, we asked Mac...we said we were a little tired sometimes of 50 percent seasons. We said, 'Why don't we have a schedule where we could look forward to [winning]. And he said 'Sure, I could give you a schedule like that.' And he named a few of the schools we could play. But he said, 'What would you rather remember, that you played on the same field as a team that played Iowa the week before in the Big 10, and maybe you lost by a touchdown,' which we did, 'Would you rather do that, or would you rather play against a bunch of set-ups just because you could have a score at the end of the game that would put you out front.' We got the idea. I mention sometimes about playing football for Eureka...and I say I played against George Russo who was eight years all-pro tackle with the Chicago Bears. This little school with the elms on the campus used to be known and admired by everyone we met as having the greatest spirit of anyone that they played.

Reagan graduated from Eureka in the spring of 1932. He had his diploma, but no idea what he wanted to do with it. He soon found the answer at a small radio station in Davenport, Iowa, where he worked as a sports announcer. One of his jobs was to broadcast Chicago Cubs games by reading Western Union dispatches over the air. The telegrams gave him only the briefest of descriptions of the game; Reagan would compensate by making up dramatic details of the action while a station engineer played recorded sounds of crowd noises and cheering to accompany Reagan's descriptions.

Reagan's radio career led to a Hollywood screen test, which led to a steady if unspectacular career in the movies. He was tall with boyish good looks and a homespun, small-town charm. In 1940, Reagan married actress Jane Wyman. The couple raised two children but would divorce in 1948. Wyman said the marriage fell apart because her husband started ignoring their family for what was a growing interest in political activism. She also found him boring. "If you ask Ron Reagan what time it is, he will tell you how to make a watch," she said.

Reagan had always been a liberal Democrat, but in 1947 he was elected president of the Screen Actors Guild and used his position to help expel communists from the union—although he was certainly a fierce defender of guild members he believed were unjustly accused by the zealous communist hunters of the era. Still, it was clear that

Reagan was growing more conservative as he guided the union into the 1950s. In 1952 and 1956, he headed the Democrats for Eisenhower organization, which was established to help elect the Republican candidate, Dwight D. Eisenhower, president.

In 1952, Reagan married Nancy Davis, a little-known actress who was the daughter of a wealthy Chicago physician. Nancy gave up her acting career to raise two children the Reagans had together. She became a member of a Southern California circle of wealthy conservative Republican women that included Betsy Bloomingdale, whose husband founded the credit card company Diners Club, and Mary Jane Wick, wife of an important California financier. Certainly, Nancy was an influence in her husband's turn to the right. So was the movie star Dick Powell, a good friend of the Reagans and a staunch Republican.

Meanwhile, Reagan's best years in film were behind him, so he turned to the then-infant medium of television, where he signed on to host General Electric Theater, a widely popular series of dramas. The job required him to tour the country acting as a celebrity spokesman for GE. It also required him to visit GE appliance factories where he met many of the company's executives—virtually all of them political

A 1927 photograph of sixteen-year-old Ronald Reagan in his uniform as a lifeguard at Lowell Park Beach, Illinois. When he was fifteen, Reagan began working summers at Lowell Park Beach, a popular swimming spot on the Rock River two miles upstream from Dixon. Its sandy shore gave way to a few yards of mud before sloping precipitously to depths where the undertow could be extremely strong. During his seven years as a lifeguard, Reagan was credited with seventy-seven rescues, several of which made the front page of the *Dixon Telegraph*. "Pulled from the Jaws of Death" was the headline on August 3, 1928. Reagan took great pride in saving lives. On a nearby log, he carved a notch for each rescue with his jackknife. "How many you got now?" Reagan would be asked. "You count 'em," he would reply. One of the "jokes" in the 1928 *Dixonian* was:

DROWNING YOUTH: "Don't rescue me. I want to die."
DUTCH REAGAN: "Well, you'll have to postpone that; I want a medal."

Reagan was paid eighteen dollars a week. He saved most of this money for anticipated college tuition. (Reagan was one of only 8 percent of his North Dixon High School graduating class of 1928 who went on to college.) "You know why I had such fun [at being a lifeguard]?" Reagan asked in his memoirs. "Because I was the only one up there on the grand stand. It was like a stage. Everyone had to look at me."

In September 1928, Reagan enrolled at Eureka College in Illinois, a small school run by the Disciples of Christ, a church whose credo his mother had embraced. A football hero of Dutch's had attended the school and his girlfriend, Margaret Cleaver, also was studying there. "I fell head over heels in love with Eureka," Reagan later wrote. "It seemed to me then, as I walked up the path, to be another home. I wanted to get into that school so badly that it hurt when I thought about it." Reagan was able to afford the tuition because he had saved several hundred dollars from his summer lifeguard job, received a partial athletic scholarship, and worked for his board by washing dishes at a local fraternity house.

Eureka College competed fiercely for football talent because a star player and a winning team attracted students. Eureka's elders disdained athletics, because the school's main commitment was to teaching a Christian doctrine. But without a competitive football team, the school lost many prospective students.

When Reagan attended the school, Eureka had an enrollment of two hundred and twenty students but it bore few resemblances to other college campuses. It was a small rural school with strict standards of student behavior. For example, dancing was not allowed.

All of the character traits that Reagan had exhibited at North Dixon High School were reinforced at Eureka College. He never was a great student. Reagan recalled that his enthusiasm was in "drama, sports, and politics and not always in that order." Reagan played first-string guard on the football team, worked on the school newspaper and yearbooks, became president of the Booster Club, was captain of the basketball cheerleaders, and appeared in most college plays, usually having the lead role.

Reagan was a feature writer for the *Prism*, Eureka's yearbook.

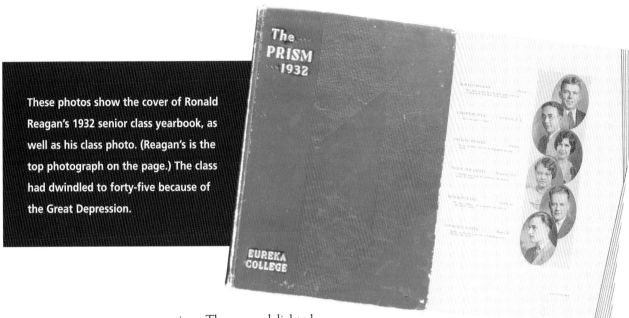

These photos show the cover of Ronald Reagan's 1932 senior class yearbook, as well as his class photo. (Reagan's is the top photograph on the page.) The class had dwindled to forty-five because of the Great Depression.

conservatives. They were delighted to share their political views with Reagan, telling him about the evils of big government and their belief that government should keep its hands off business. By the early 1960s, Reagan was committed to the cause of conservatism.

In 1966, he answered an invitation by California Republicans to run for governor. He overwhelmed the state's Democratic governor that fall, beginning a political career that culminated in his election as president in 1980. That year, he ran against President Jimmy Carter, who was unable to solve the nation's severe economic problems. Carter also fell out of favor with the American people because he had been unable to negotiate the release of U.S. hostages captured in an embassy takeover by fundamentalist Muslim students in Tehran, Iran.

Preaching a distrust of big government as well as a promise to turn America into a strong military force, Reagan was elected in a landslide over Carter, and then easily won reelection four years later. He made good on his promise to make the United States into a military power of unprecedented might. The Reagan arms build-up was so successful that it is regarded as a main factor leading to the collapse of the Soviet Union.

Reagan remained immensely popular with the American people throughout his presidency. He never forgot the values he learned growing up in a small town or attending college on a tiny campus. Returning to Eureka to make a speech, Reagan said, "Those big assembly-line diploma mills may teach…but you will have memories, you will have friendships that are impossible on those great campuses, and just are peculiar to this place….Yes, this place is deep in my heart. Everything that has been good in my life began here."

—Hal Marcovitz

George H. W. Bush
Chapter Forty

H enry L. Stimson graduated from Phillips Academy in Andover,
Massachusetts, in 1883, and from there went on to a busy career in
public service. By 1942, when he was invited back to Andover to be
the commencement speaker for that year's graduating class, Stimson was serving
as secretary of war under President Franklin D. Roosevelt.

By then, the world was at war. The previous December, Japanese planes
launched from a naval task force had attacked the U.S. Navy base at Pearl Harbor
in Hawaii, sinking eighteen U.S. ships, destroying two hundred airplanes, and
killing or wounding more than three thousand servicemen. The surprise attack led
to the United States's involvement in World War II. When Stimson addressed
Andover's Class of 1942, America was preparing for a long conflict and desperately
needed young, able-bodied men to take up arms.

During his address to the Andover graduates, Stimson told the boys that a
soldier should be "brave without being brutal, self-confident without boasting, part
of an irresistible might, but without losing faith in individual liberty." Nevertheless,
Stimson counseled the Andover graduates to stay in school and begin their college
educations before joining the armed forces.

One of the graduates in the audience that day was George H. W. Bush. The
previous December, he had been stunned by the surprise attack on Pearl Harbor and
resolved then to enlist in the Navy at the earliest opportunity. Although George
had been accepted at Yale University, he aimed to be a Navy pilot and decided
college could wait. His parents, teachers, and now even Secretary Stimson urged
him to change his mind, but George was steadfast in his plan to enlist.

Shortly after commencement exercises concluded George's parents, Prescott
and Dorothy Bush, encountered their son in the hallway of Andover's Cochran
Chapel. Prescott asked George whether Stimson's words had changed his mind. "No
sir," George responded. "I'm going in."

Prescott shook hands with his son, and then began to cry.

A few days later, George Bush celebrated his eighteenth birthday by going to

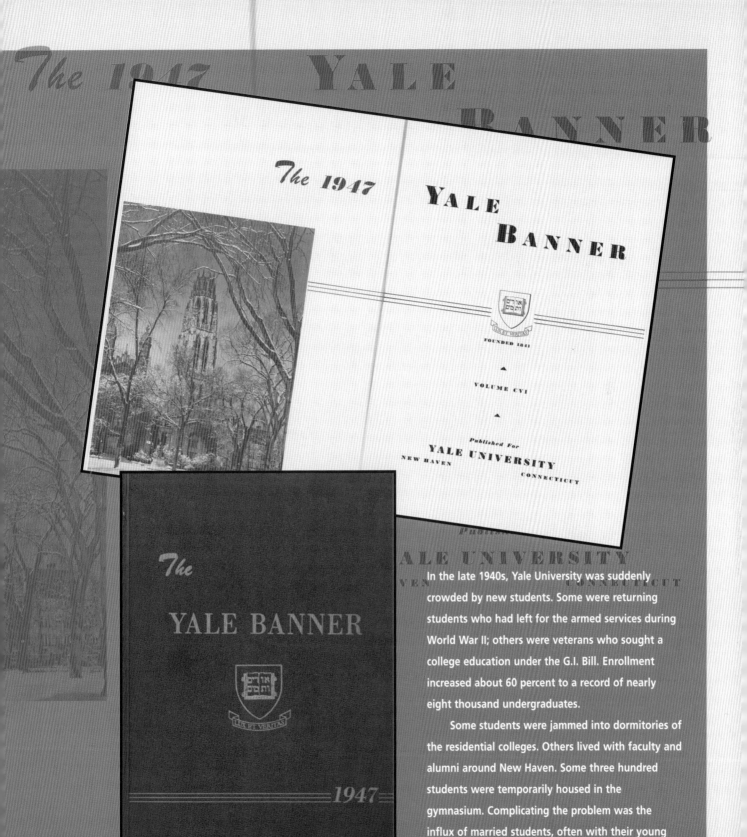

In the late 1940s, Yale University was suddenly crowded by new students. Some were returning students who had left for the armed services during World War II; others were veterans who sought a college education under the G.I. Bill. Enrollment increased about 60 percent to a record of nearly eight thousand undergraduates.

Some students were jammed into dormitories of the residential colleges. Others lived with faculty and alumni around New Haven. Some three hundred students were temporarily housed in the gymnasium. Complicating the problem was the influx of married students, often with their young children. To house them, one hundred Quonset huts were rapidly erected near the Yale Bowl. Each of the forty-eight-by-twenty-foot metal structures was divided into two three-room apartments.

CAPT. G.H.W. BUSH '48

George H. W. Bush, wearing his baseball uniform, sits on the Yale Fence. For generations, Yale students sat on the fence at the corner of Chapel and College Streets. Each class, except freshmen, had a specific place where they perched themselves, smoked, laughed, chatted, and sang together. Being photographed "sitting on the fence" is a Yale tradition.

Although George had been accepted at Yale University, he aimed to be a Navy pilot and decided college could wait.

the U.S. Navy recruitment office in Boston and enlisting as a seaman second class. By that summer he was enrolled in aviator cadet school in North Carolina.

George Bush was far from the most academically talented student at Andover. He was athletic, to be sure, but there were better athletes at Andover. But no boy at Andover beat him to the recruitment office, and no member of the Andover Class of 1942 would accomplish as much in combat as George Bush.

George Herbert Walker Bush was born on June 12, 1924, in Milton, Massachusetts, where his family was living temporarily while Prescott Bush worked as an executive for a rubber products company. There was wealth on both sides of young George's family. The Bushes were distant relatives of King Henry III of Great Britain, making George a thirteenth cousin of Queen Elizabeth II. Prescott was the son of Samuel Bush, who had made a fortune as a manufacturer of parts and equipment for railroad cars. Samuel sent his children to private schools and the best colleges. Prescott graduated from Yale and, after making his mark as an executive with a talent for rescuing troubled companies, turned to investment banking and later politics. In 1952, he was elected to the U.S. Senate representing Connecticut, where the family had moved soon after George's birth.

George's mother was also born into wealth. She was the daughter of George Herbert Walker, whose ancestors had emigrated to America in the early seventeenth century. By the time Dorothy Walker married Prescott Bush, the Walkers were the owners of one of the nation's largest dry goods companies and

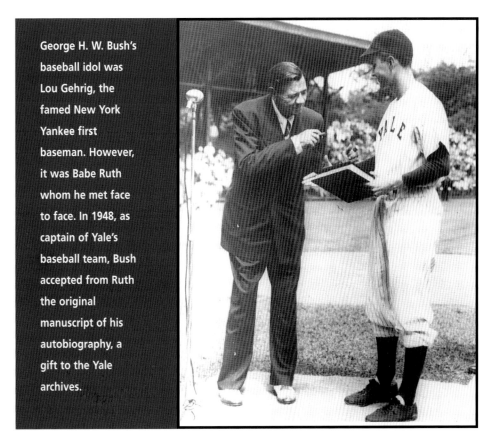

George H. W. Bush's baseball idol was Lou Gehrig, the famed New York Yankee first baseman. However, it was Babe Ruth whom he met face to face. In 1948, as captain of Yale's baseball team, Bush accepted from Ruth the original manuscript of his autobiography, a gift to the Yale archives.

George Herbert Walker was president of a prosperous New York investment banking firm. Dorothy Walker and her family spent their summers in a seaside home in Kennebunkport, Maine, and their winter vacations in a shooting lodge in South Carolina known as Duncannon.

George Bush was the second of five children born to Prescott and Dorothy. George's older brother, Prescott Jr., was called "Pressy" by everyone in the family. George had a nickname, too. He was called "Poppy," an unusual nickname for a little boy. He came by the nickname because the children called Grandfather George "Pop." George was, then, "Little Pop," and soon simply "Poppy."

George Bush grew up in Greenwich, a wealthy Connecticut suburb of New York City. The Bush children spent their childhoods amid mansions, estates, and servants. In 1929, the American stock market crashed, plunging the country into an economic catastrophe known as the Great Depression. Hundreds of thousands of people were thrown out of work, and many found themselves standing in lines for bread. In the Midwest, thousands of citizens of Oklahoma and other Plains states were forced to give up their homes when their crops failed. To George Bush and the other privileged children who grew up in Greenwich in the 1920s and 1930s, however, that world was far-removed and virtually unknown.

There were twenty public schools in Greenwich when George was growing up. He would never set foot in any of them, at least not as a student. George Bush began his education at the age of five when his parents enrolled him in the private Greenwich Country Day School. The school was located on the estate of the Warner family of Greenwich and sprawled over some eighteen acres. His parents wanted to wait until he was six before sending him off to school, but Pressy, who was twenty-one months older than George, was already going to school and George complained that he was lonely at home without his brother.

Each morning, the Bush family chauffeur dropped Prescott Sr. off at the Greenwich train station for his commute into New York, then stopped by Greenwich Country Day School to let Pressy and Poppy out for classes. Later, the chauffeur made another stop—at Rosemary Junior School, the private girls' school in Greenwich where sister Nancy attended. At the time, Greenwich Country was an all-boys school.

The school day was long. It commenced at 8:30 A.M. and lasted until 6 P.M. Ordinarily, children are dismissed from school in the mid-afternoon and can be expected to spend the remainder of their afternoons playing together in their neighborhoods, doing their chores, or working in after-school jobs. There were no "neighborhoods" in Greenwich where children could meet after school for games of stickball or marbles, however, and children from wealthy families did not need jobs to earn extra money. Also, parents were rarely home in the afternoons to supervise their children's play. Greenwich Country Day School was charged with looking after its students long after most public school children had been dismissed from classes.

TORCH

University Honor Society
FOUNDED 1916

GEORGE HERBERT W. BUSH
JOHN CLARK CALHOUN, JR.
CHARLES HALSEY CLARK
WILLIAM JUDKINS CLARK
ENDICOTT PEABODY DAVISON
EUGENE DINES, JR.
WINTHROP PALMER ELDREDGE
WILLIAM RICHARD EMERSON
GORDON NESBITT FARQUHAR
RICHARD ELWOOD JENKINS

VANDERVEER KIRK
ROBERT PERKINS KNIGHT
ARTHUR KEEFE MOHER
THOMAS WILDER MOSELEY
FRANK O'BRIEN, JR.
JOHN JOSEPH O'NEILL
GEORGE HAROLD PFAU, JR.
JOHN GRANDIN ROHRBACH
DAVID OWEN WAGSTER
SAMUEL SLOANE WALKER, JR.

HOWARD SAYRE WEAVER

Back Row: Emerson, Farquhar, Clark, C. H., Bush, Clark, W. S., Wagster, Walker.
Second Row: Pfau, Knight, Weaver, Dines, Moseley, Rohrbach, Moher.
Front Row: O'Brien, Calhoun, Kirk, Davison, Eldredge.

63

This page from the 1947 Yale yearbook shows the members of the Yale Honors Society. George Bush is in the center of the back row.

Bush was also selected as a member of a more exclusive organization. Yale's Skull and Bones, founded in 1833, was (and remains) a secret intellectual and fraternal society. The Bonesmen met in padlocked windowless rooms that were filled with the same sorts of knickknacks and worn leather chairs found in the old clubs of an English university. Bonesmen were required to leave a room if they ever heard the words "Skull and Bones" uttered by non-members. Likewise, Bonesmen were forbidden even to say the name in conversation with those who were not members. Each year, fifteen graduating members of this exclusive group were replaced by an equal number of inductees.

For George H. W. Bush, being tapped for Skull and Bones was a thrill that he had long dreamt about. His father had been a Bonesman, as had other relatives and family friends. Bush's Skull and Bones contemporaries became his lifelong friends. They formed a core of a network that assisted his future career both in business and in politics.

George and the one hundred and forty other Greenwich students wore uniforms—knickers as well as black sweaters with orange stripes on the sleeves. Poppy Bush and his classmates studied history, geography, mathematics, English, Latin, music, nature studies, and art. Athletics were stressed—students played baseball, soccer and, when the pond froze over in the winter, ice hockey.

Discipline was strict, particularly under George Meadows, an Englishman who became headmaster in 1936. He was very tough on miscreants who talked during assembly, making them stand on their chairs until dismissed, and gum-chewers, who were sentenced to eat a whole pack of gum while standing at attention in front of the student body.

George remained at Greenwich until the spring of 1937, and then enrolled at Phillips Academy in the fall of that year. By setting foot onto the Andover campus he entered one of the nation's most prestigious private boarding schools. Children who attend the school, known familiarly as Andover, are expected to go on to careers in law, literature, the arts, or business. Among the graduates of Andover are actors Jack Lemmon and Humphrey Bogart, artist Frank Stella, photographer Walker Evans, author Edgar Rice Burroughs, and inventor Samuel F. B. Morse. Noted journalists, as well as members of Congress, governors, and justices of the U.S. Supreme Court, have attended Andover as well.

The school, which is located twenty-one miles north of Boston, was founded in 1778 by Samuel Phillips Jr. Paul Revere designed the school seal while John Hancock, then serving as governor of Massachusetts, signed Andover's incorporation papers. The school's charter admonishes its students to understand that "goodness without knowledge is weak…yet knowledge without goodness is dangerous."

When George Bush commenced his education at Andover, the Great Depression still hovered over the lives of ordinary Americans. At Andover, though, Bush was just as shielded from the horrors of poverty as he had been back home in Greenwich. In fact, students were instructed not to leave campus for visits to the town of Andover, just past the school's border.

President Franklin Roosevelt was held very much in disdain by the faculty, administrators, and even the students of Andover. Roosevelt, the son of a wealthy New York family, had grown up in circumstances similar to the average Andover

> Bush excelled more on the athletic field than he did in the classrooms at Andover. He was one of the tallest boys in school, and played basketball, soccer, and baseball.

student, yet around the Andover campus his liberal New Deal programs were despised. Roosevelt's New Deal used government funding—and, therefore, the taxes paid by the wealthy—in an attempt to pull the United States out of the Depression. At Andover the student newspaper, the *Phillipian*, referred to Roosevelt as a "betrayer of his class."

George Bush may have agreed with the editorial policy of the *Phillipian*, but at the time he was not in the habit of sharing his views publicly. During the five years he spent at Andover, George joined many extracurricular clubs, both social and academic, but throughout that time he displayed a nonchalant attitude toward politics and social activism. Bush became a very popular boy on campus mostly because he had a talent for staying out of scrapes. He was friendly with everybody, earning their respect because of his pleasant nature and sense of humor. His teachers liked him because he was well behaved.

He never impressed his teachers with his academic prowess. Although he did not lack intelligence—in college, he would make Phi Beta Kappa—his teachers at Andover recalled that George was for the most part a mediocre student. "His grades in my course were not very good," said Andover teacher Hart Day Leavitt. "He was in my eleventh-grade English class, but my remaining impression is he just sat in the class and handed in his papers."

Bush excelled more, though, on the athletic field. He was one of the tallest boys in school—by his senior year he was already standing six feet tall. He played basketball, soccer, and baseball. He was elected captain of the soccer and baseball teams because he was the most enthusiastic member of the teams, and his teammates found themselves infected with his enthusiasm.

"He was a very well-liked kid," recalled Frank DiClemente, the Andover physical education teacher and baseball coach. "You never heard that guy say anything bad about anybody. If he had anything to say about a person, it would be in a positive sense."

Even the outbreak of World War II didn't seem to dampen George's enthusiasm. On campus, Headmaster Claude Moore Fuess convened a special assembly to report the news of the Japanese attack to the student body. Bush was a member of the senior class, and he was planning to enroll at Yale after graduating the following spring. During that assembly, though, he resolved to enlist in the Navy.

During Christmas vacation that winter, George returned home to Greenwich and attended a dance at the Round Hill Country Club. At the dance he met a sixteen-year-old girl named Barbara Pierce, who was soon to become his fiancée. She was a student at an exclusive girls' prep school in Charleston, South Carolina, and was home for the holidays as well. Barbara Pierce's mother, Pauline Robinson Pierce, was the daughter of an Ohio Supreme Court justice. Her father, Marvin Pierce, was a magazine publisher and descendant of former U.S. president Franklin Pierce.

George H. W. Bush and Barbara Pierce married in January 1945. He was not yet twenty-one and she was a year younger. In September, Bush entered all-male Yale University. Veterans comprised more than half of his class—and one-quarter of them were married with wives living in New Haven. On July 6, 1946, Barbara gave birth to their first child, whom they named George Walker Bush.

At Yale, as well as at every major college, veterans assisted by government benefits under the G.I. Bill changed the traditional campus scene. The Bushes were fortunate to live in an apartment with a shared kitchen within a sprawling house on New Haven's Hillhouse Avenue. The house had been subdivided into thirteen separate apartments.

In these cramped quarters, Bush studied and helped raise his infant son. He majored in business and economics. In his senior year, Bush won the Gordon Brown Prize for "all around student leadership" and he was elected to Phi Beta Kappa, the national undergraduate honor society.

These photographs show George Bush holding his infant son in their New Haven home (top) and George W. on his father's shoulders (left). Both were taken in April 1947.

Following the holidays, George returned to Andover while Barbara went back to Charleston. They kept in touch by writing letters. That spring, George graduated from Andover and kept his promise to himself to enlist in the navy. On August 6, 1942, he reported for duty in Chapel Hill, North Carolina, where he began training as an aviation cadet.

At the start of the war, the navy declared that a would-be pilot needed at least two years of college to be considered for aviator training. The Battle of Midway changed the navy's thinking. Fought in early June of 1942—just as Bush was accepting his diploma at Andover—Midway became the first significant naval aviation battle of the war. The battle was fought in the skies over the Midway Islands by planes launched from Japanese and American aircraft carriers. (The two enemy fleets never came into contact with one another.) American air power prevailed, delivering a blow to Japan's attempts to seize the islands and stage a future invasion of Hawaii. Nevertheless, the battle convinced the U.S. Navy that it needed pilots, and there would be too few available if two years of college was a prerequisite. The college rule was waived, opening the doors to aviation cadet school to high school graduates.

Bush would undergo pilot training for some eighteen months. His training took him to seven navy bases and included stopovers in North Carolina, Minnesota, Texas, Florida, Massachusetts, Rhode Island, and Virginia. During that time, he learned to fly a torpedo bomber called the Avenger—a single-engine plane designed to take off from an aircraft carrier and deliver a torpedo or depth charges aimed at an enemy target. The training was grueling and hazardous. Bush had to learn how to perform takeoffs and landings from the deck of a carrier, which pitched and heaved in choppy ocean waters. What's more, many of those carrier maneuvers had to be performed at night when visibility was low.

"One can practice carrier landings on land forever without knowing the thrill of actually landing on a moving ship at sea," Bush said years later. "There's something about the isolation, the ocean, the tiny carrier below that gets the adrenaline flowing."

On June 6, 1943, George Bush was commissioned an ensign in the U.S. Navy. He was issued a set of gold wings that were pinned to his uniform designating him a naval aviator. Bush, who had not yet turned nineteen, was at the time the youngest pilot in the U.S. Navy. After more training he was assigned in February 1944 to a squadron of torpedo bombers aboard the U.S.S. *San Jacinto*, a newly commissioned aircraft carrier dispatched to duty in the South Pacific.

By the time the war was over George Bush had flown fifty-eight missions, logging 1,228 hours as a military pilot. He made one hundred and twenty-six carrier landings. He was shot down twice, but managed to escape injury and capture, and was awarded the Distinguished Flying Cross—the military's highest award for valor by a pilot. In August 1945 the war ended after the United States unleashed atomic bombs on the Japanese cities of Hiroshima and Nagasaki. Less than a month later, George Bush received an honorable discharge from the U.S. Navy.

George Bush had married Barbara the previous winter. Now, he was anxious to get on with his education. He enrolled in Yale for the fall 1945 semester. The couple found an apartment in New Haven, Connecticut. Bush took up the study of business and economics. He was in the largest freshman class in the history of the college, a fact attributed to the massive discharge of men from the armed services and the government's commitment to help pay for their college educations through the G.I. Bill of Rights.

Bush made Phi Beta Kappa at Yale and completed the requirements for what is ordinarily a four-year degree in three years. The easygoing, friendly attitude that made him popular at Andover also made him many friends at Yale. In Yale's case, his friends turned out to be very influential because Bush was invited to join Skull and Bones.

Fraternities and sororities are very common on college campuses. Many of them have their roots in the literary societies of colonial days—clubs composed of students who met on their own, outside the influence of the faculty, to practice their writing and oratory skills. Over the years, many such groups have adopted customs and rituals they prefer to keep secret. Perhaps no group has maintained the custom of secrecy with such dedication as Yale's Skull and Bones. The members, known as Bonesmen, meet in a windowless clubhouse known as the Tomb, which is located on High Street in New Haven. The club was established in 1832. Its members have included Supreme Court justice Potter Stewart, President William Howard Taft, *Time* magazine publisher Henry Luce, journalist William F. Buckley Jr., and U.S. senator John F. Chafee.

Each year, fifteen Yale men are asked to join. Women are barred from membership. Whatever goes on behind the doors of the Tomb is, of course, a closely guarded secret. Nevertheless, for years following their experiences at New Haven, Bonesmen regard themselves as members of a select group, always ready to come to the aid of one another. Soon after Bush left Yale, a fellow Bonesmen named Neil Mallon would give him his start in the oil exploration business in Texas.

Other than Skull and Bones, Bush's other great passion on the Yale campus was the baseball team. Once again, his teammates elected him captain. He played first base and was regarded as a gifted fielder. When the Yale baseball team won two regional championships during his two years on the team, pro scouts stopped by to see if any members of the team were worthy of major league contracts. The team's sure-handed first baseman caught their eye until they saw his batting average—a paltry .239 his first year, a respectable but hardly impressive .269 in his second season.

George Bush graduated from Yale in the spring of 1948. He would pursue a career in the oil business in Texas, switching to politics in the 1960s. He served two terms in the U.S. House of Representatives and was appointed by Republican administrations to posts that included ambassador to the United Nations, special envoy to China, and director of the Central Intelligence Agency.

In 1980, he campaigned for president and ran a strong second in the Republican primaries to eventual nominee Ronald Reagan, who asked him to join the ticket as the party's vice presidential candidate. Bush spent eight years as Reagan's vice president, then was elected president in 1988. His single term in office was marked by his decision to wage war in the Persian Gulf to drive an invading Iraqi army out of neighboring Kuwait. Although victory in the 1991 Gulf War boosted Bush's popularity, his inability to revive the country's sagging economy led to his defeat at the hands of Democrat Bill Clinton in the 1992 election.

He left active politics following his loss to Clinton, but in January 2001 he stood by his son, George W. Bush, as the former governor of Texas—who had followed his father to Andover and Yale—took the oath of office as the nation's forty-third president. The two Bushes became the first father and son to serve as presidents since John Adams and John Quincy Adams two centuries ago.

—Hal Marcovitz

Bill Clinton

Chapter Forty-one

In the summer of 1963, when Bill Clinton was sixteen years old, he
participated in Boys' Nation, a weeklong convention in Washington, D.C.,
meant to teach young people about the government of the United States. For
Clinton and the other Boys' Nation "senators," the trip would involve more than
just sight-seeing tours of landmarks and government buildings. The American
Legion, which sponsored the event, expected the boys to elect officers, participate
in debates, and take votes on resolutions that would address many of the same
issues faced by Congress.

To take part in Boys' Nation, Bill Clinton won the position of senator at his
home state's convention at an Arkansas summer camp. He spent the week
campaigning, going from cabin to cabin each night so he could introduce himself to
the hundreds of boys in attendance. Each morning, he rose early and stationed
himself at the entrance of the cafeteria where he shook hands with the boys as they
arrived for breakfast. He recruited many friends at the camp, and they fanned out
and urged their friends to vote for Bill Clinton for Boys' Nation senator.

Bill Clinton was a born campaigner. He won the election in a landslide.

William Jefferson Blythe III was born on August 19, 1946. His father, Bill
Blythe Jr., died in a car accident three months before his son's birth. When Bill was
two years old, his mother Virginia decided she needed an education in nursing in
order to support her son. She made the sacrifice of living away from him for the
next two years, attending nursing school in New Orleans and sending Bill to live
with her parents, Elbridge and Edith Cassidy, in their home in Hope, Arkansas, a
tiny town near the Texas border.

It was Edith Cassidy who first recognized the boy's intelligence. Under her
guidance, Bill learned to read before he was three years old. "From the beginning,
Bill was a special child—smart, sensitive, mature beyond his years," recalled
Virginia. "He remembers my sitting him down in that house on Thirteenth Street
and telling him about his real father. He must have been four or five at the time,
but talking with him at that age was like talking with a grown friend."

Bill learned to read before he was three years old. "From the beginning, Bill was a special child—smart, sensitive, mature beyond his years," his mother recalled.

Bill Clinton attended Hot Springs High School, 1960–64. During the summer between his junior and senior years, Clinton participated in Boys' Nation, an American Legion–sponsored program to help students learn about the U.S. government and its operation. For Clinton, the highlight of the program was a visit to the White House, where President John F. Kennedy greeted the group. Clinton was in the front, so when Kennedy finished his prepared remarks and stepped forward to greet the delegates, the first hand the president clasped was that of sixteen-year-old Bill Clinton. Later in his life, Clinton often said that this was the moment he decided on a political career.

This photograph ranks among the most popular requested from the White House during Clinton's years as president.

WM. J. CLINTON
FS 1968

A REALISTIC APPROACH
TO
STUDENT GOVERNMENT

BILL CLINTON

CANDIDATE

PRESIDENT OF THE STUDENT COUNCIL

MAR. 8 1967

Georgetown, the nation's oldest Roman Catholic university, was founded in 1789. The school was the idea of John Carroll, the first Catholic bishop in the United States and the first archbishop of Baltimore. His goal was to establish a college so that young Catholic men would no longer be compelled to go abroad for a higher education. Their alternative was to matriculate at the non-sectarian University of Pennsylvania, which alone among America's colleges welcomed Catholics. The Georgetown curriculum was modeled on that of the typical classical academy. Georgetown has always been open to students of all religious faiths. George Washington's two nephews attended the school in the late 1790s.

In 1919, the university inaugurated the Georgetown School of Foreign Service to train students who intended to enter diplomatic service or become employees of corporations involved in international business. Bill Clinton, who graduated fourth in his high school class of three hundred and sixty-three students, chose to attend Georgetown because of the university's School of Foreign Service. His goal was to combine the practical experience of working for a member of Congress with the more regimented course work of the college. The nation's capital and Georgetown promised academic challenge, social excitement, and political possibility.

Bill Clinton entered Georgetown University in 1964. Clinton's easy-going manner, coupled with his intelligence, charm, and sincerity, overcame any reservations his more affluent classmates may have felt about the economically underprivileged boy from one of the poorest states in the nation. Recalling those days, Clinton said, "I'd never been out of Arkansas really very much, and there I was with people from all over the country and all over the world." Those people must have liked Clinton because they elected him president of his freshman and sophomore classes.

While at Georgetown, Clinton always held at least one part-time job to supplement his family's financial support. He was able to juggle many activities and still maintain a 3.57 grade-point average.

Meanwhile, Virginia met car salesman Roger Clinton. Roger loved to gamble and roam the bars in search of fun. Virginia thought she could tame his wild spirit, and they married in 1950. Roger and Virginia Clinton and Virginia's son Bill moved into a small house in Hope.

Virginia enrolled her boy in school as Bill Clinton, a name Bill would legally adopt at the age of fifteen to form a bond with his younger stepbrother, Roger Clinton Jr. From early on, Bill impressed his teachers will his eagerness to learn. Some of his teachers weren't quite sure what to make of the boy who always knew the answers. In the second grade, he raised his hand so much that his teacher regarded him as a pest and gave him a "D" in behavior. That would be Bill's last poor grade. For the rest of his school years he was an "A" student who seemed far ahead of his classmates.

Roger Sr. was originally from the Arkansas city of Hot Springs, and that's where the family moved in 1952. Bill's stepfather lost money in the car business in Hope and decided to give it up and try farming. The family found a farm on the edge of Hot Springs, but it became clear that Roger Clinton was not the type of man who could drag himself out of bed to milk the cows. Roger enjoyed the nightlife too much to keep farmers' hours. Virginia had no intentions of becoming a farm wife, either. By now she had become a nurse-anesthetist, and found her skills in demand by Hot Springs surgeons. After just a few months, the Clintons moved to a home on Park Avenue in Hot Springs, and Roger Clinton found a job as a salesman.

Bill's interest in politics and government may have started as early as the summer of 1956, just after he completed the fourth grade. That year, the political conventions were being televised and Bill found himself much more interested in the intrigues and dramas unfolding on the floors of the convention halls than in such typical childhood television fare as *Howdy Doody* and the *Mickey Mouse Club.* "I was hooked on politics then and there," Clinton said later. "It got to me in a way on television that no amount of reading in the newspapers about candidates running for office and politics in general could impact me."

Most people in Hot Springs were Republicans. Bill was an independent thinker, though, and as he grew older he became partial to the Democratic Party's liberal politics. In 1960, as a student at Central Junior High School in Hot Springs, Clinton closely followed the presidential election pitting Republican Vice President Richard M. Nixon against the young Democratic senator from Massachusetts, John F. Kennedy.

"My teacher in ninth-grade civics class was Mary Marty, and she had the class debating the merits of the two candidates for the White House," Clinton recalled. "Mrs. Marty and I were the only ones who were for the [Kennedy] ticket. Being that Hot Springs is the seat of government for Garland County and is heavily Republican, my teacher and I were like outcasts in an environment that had everyone else rooting for Nixon."

On November 8, 1960, fourteen-year-old Bill Clinton stayed up all night watching the election returns on TV. "What a rewarding moment it was for me when Nixon made his concession speech," Bill said.

Bill Clinton soon entered Hot Springs High School. He was clearly one of the brightest students in school. What's more, he was a natural leader. Bill joined many school clubs and held numerous leadership positions; he won his first election in 1961 when his classmates voted him president of the sophomore class.

At home, though, things were not going as well. Bill's stepfather was an alcoholic who abused Virginia. There were many angry confrontations between his parents; Bill would shut himself off in his room to escape the fighting. Bill had taken up the saxophone and would often rely on the instrument to help him escape the raucous fighting elsewhere in the house, practicing music to drown out the voices of Virginia and Roger.

When Bill arrived at Hot Springs High School his talent was recognized by Virgil Spurlin, the music teacher and band director. Spurlin appointed Bill the band major, a job that went to the school's most accomplished musician. Spurlin recognized Bill's intelligence and popularity and knew he would be a vast help in organizing the annual Arkansas statewide band competition, which Hot Springs High School hosted. The festival featured performances by one hundred and forty high school bands from throughout Arkansas.

Clinton worked hard to help Spurlin coordinate the festival while still finding time to practice and compete with the Hot Springs High School band himself. He also joined the Stardusters, the Hot Springs dance band. Clinton and some friends also formed a jazz combo that played in the high school cafeteria during lunch hour. They wore dark sunglasses, which prompted their classmates to call the group the Three Blind Mice. At home, the walls of his bedroom displayed the numerous medals and awards he received for winning saxophone competitions. By the time he entered his senior year in high school, he was being urged by his teachers to major in music at college.

Spurlin recalled, "One time down in Camden, Arkansas, I believe he was in a stage band, and he was a soloist, and he received the outstanding soloist for the state in this particular case. And it wasn't just the fact that he was an accomplished musician, but he had to read music of all kinds of moods and different kinds of music, from jazz to classical to everything in the book, and he just did a phenomenal job in that."

As tempting as the idea of a career in music seemed, in the summer of 1963 Bill was picked to attend Boys' Nation, where he made up his mind to pursue a career in politics and government. Bill Clinton left for Boys' Nation on July 19, 1963. For the next week, Bill and the other senators lived in dormitories at the University of Maryland. Their days were filled with trips to Cabinet departments, lunches with members of Congress and sessions to draft resolutions that would be placed before all one hundred Boys' Nation senators for a vote.

In the summer of 1963, the rights of African Americans were still very much in dispute. In 1962, President Kennedy had been forced to send United States marshals to Mississippi so that a black student, James Meredith, could be admitted to the all-white University of Mississippi. Eight months later, Kennedy sent U.S. marshals as well as federal troops to the University of Alabama to ensure that two black students would be permitted to enroll there.

The Boys' Nation senators drafted a resolution supporting civil rights for African Americans. Bill was one of the major voices for civil rights at the convention. He worked hard rounding up votes for the civil rights resolution, using the same political skills that had won him votes just a few weeks before at the state convention in Little Rock.

He found opposition on the convention floor. Two of the southern senators— Pete Johnson of Alabama and Tommy Lawhorne of Georgia—were committed to defeating the civil rights resolution. One morning, they confronted Bill in the University of Maryland cafeteria. They told Bill that the southern senators had to stick together to defeat the resolution. Soon, Bill and the other two boys were shouting at one another. Bill refused to budge, though, and Johnson and Lawhorne had to back off. Ultimately, the civil rights resolution won by a small margin.

The next morning, the senators boarded buses on the University of Maryland campus for what was to be the final activity—a tour of the White House and a meeting with President Kennedy.

When the other boys showed up to board the buses, they found Bill already standing in line. He had arrived first because he intended to sit in the front seat of the first bus so that he could be first off the bus. That way, Bill was sure he could be first to meet the president. When the buses arrived at the White House Bill leaped out of his seat and hurried to the front of the line. He found a place just to the right of where Kennedy was expected to stand on the White House lawn to greet the boys.

Just before ten o'clock in the morning, Kennedy stepped out of the White House to address the Boys' Nation senators. He told them that he had read a newspaper story that morning about their convention and was impressed with their resolution calling for civil rights. When he concluded his speech, the president stepped forward and extended his hand to greet the senators. The first hand he shook was Bill Clinton's.

Bill graduated from Hot Springs High School in May 1964. He was neither valedictorian nor salutatorian, but his grades placed him fourth in the class, and he was picked to deliver the benediction, typically a brief prayer to close the ceremony. Bill turned it into a rousing salute to the graduates, challenging them to do their best in life. "Lord, make us care so that we will never know the misery and muddle of a life without purpose, and so that when we die, others will still have the opportunity to live in a free land," he told his three hundred and sixty-two fellow graduates.

There was no question where Bill intended to go to college—the nation's capital. He picked Georgetown University and enrolled in the college's School of Foreign Service, drawn to a curriculum that would train him for a future in the service of his national government. From the moment Bill stepped on campus that fall, he was off and running in a college election. He launched a vigorous campaign for president of the freshman class. He developed a platform and staged a rally, complete with a makeshift band composed of college students, and was easily elected president. After the election, Georgetown's student magazine reported, "Bill Clinton, who looks and sounds like an amiable farm boy, is the latest to ascend to the position of status supremacy known as freshman class president."

Bill was a top student at Georgetown, taking courses in political science, philosophy, and comparative cultures. He also became active in the anti-war movement. With opposition to the Vietnam War growing, many college students took part in anti-war demonstrations and opposed the Selective Service, the draft that required young men to enter the military and fight in Vietnam. On October 21, 1967, Bill was one of 55,000 people who attended an anti-war march that ended at the Lincoln Memorial. The next spring, Bill campaigned for U.S. senator Robert F. Kennedy, whose presidential campaign called for American withdrawal from Southeast Asia.

While attending Georgetown, Bill won a part-time job on the staff of the Senate Foreign Relations Committee, which was headed by Senator J. William Fulbright, an Arkansas Democrat. The young college student and the scholarly senator from Arkansas would form a bond stemming from that experience, and in the future Fulbright would mentor Bill as his political career began to rise.

Bill worked as a clerk in the committee's documents room. His duties included sorting mail and filing reports, clipping stories about foreign relations from daily newspapers and running errands for committee members. For Clinton, by now an avowed political junkie, it was like working in Disneyland.

Just after starting work for Fulbright's committee, Bill wrote to his grandmother Edith Cassidy: "It is of course exciting to be here around all the senators and already this year I've seen the president....There's not much time to do anything but study and work, but I love being busy and hard work is good for people."

In April 1968, just before Bill graduated from Georgetown, civil rights leader Martin Luther King Jr. was assassinated in Memphis, Tennessee. The assassination touched off rioting in many American cities, including Washington. Bill volunteered to work for the American Red Cross, driving food into riot-torn Washington neighborhoods because commercial truckers refused to deliver supplies to grocery stores. The organization painted a large red cross onto Bill's white Buick, which he used to make the deliveries. Carolyn Staley, a friend from Hot Springs, helped Bill make some of the deliveries. "It was very dangerous," she recalled. "We raced through red lights and all. But Bill just had to be there. Before we left the shelter, we were advised to pull hats and scarves over our faces because we were

In 1968, Bill Clinton was awarded a Rhodes Scholarship to attend Oxford University in England, one of the world's oldest and most prestigious universities. A 1901 bequest of Cecil Rhodes established these scholarships for the purpose of promoting unity among English-speaking nations. Until 1976, candidates had to be unmarried males between the ages of nineteen and twenty-five. It was Rhodes' wish that, while at Oxford, the scholars would choose instruction at the various colleges comprising the university in accordance with their own interests.

The card pictured here shows the Arms of the Colleges at Oxford University.

After studying at Oxford, Clinton entered the Yale University Law School in 1971. Even though he received a full scholarship, Clinton held various part-time jobs. He taught at a local community college, researched civil suits for a New Haven law firm, and worked briefly for a local city councilman. Clinton had little difficulty with his course work. Friends recalled how he could miss lectures, but borrow their notes to prepare for his exams by studying the night before.

ARMS OF THE COLLEGES OF OXFORD

EXETER — FOUNDED A·D·1314
JESUS COLL — FOUNDED A·D·1571
LINCOLN — FOUNDED A·D·1427
ST JOHNS — FOUNDED A·D·1555
PEMBROKE — FOUNDED A·D·1624
WORCESTER — FOUNDED A·D·1714
CORPUS CHRISTI — FOUNDED A·D·1516
NEW COLL — FOUNDED A·D·1386
WADHAM — FOUNDED A·D·1613
OXFORD UNIVERSITY — Dominus illuminatio mea
ALL SOULS — FOUNDED A·D·1437
CHRIST CHURCH — FOUNDED A·D·1546
KEBLE — FOUNDED A·D·1870
MERTON — FOUNDED A·D·1264
UNIVERSITY — FOUNDED A·D·872
QUEENS — FOUNDED A·D·1340
BALLIOL — FOUNDED A·D·1263
HERTFORD — FOUNDED A·D·1874
MAGDALEN — FOUNDED A·D·1458
ORIEL — FOUNDED A·D·1326
BRASENOSE — FOUNDED A·D·1509
TRINITY — FOUNDED A·D·1554

white. We got out and walked throughout the city and saw the burning, the looting, and were very much brought into face-to-face significance with what was going on."

During his final few months at Georgetown, Bill applied for admission to Oxford University in England on a Rhodes Scholarship. He had been urged to make the application by Senator Fulbright, himself a Rhodes scholar in 1924. The honor is awarded to thirty-two American men and women to study at Oxford for up to three years and is considered a prestigious honor.

It took more than good grades to earn the Rhodes Scholarship. Clinton was an "A" student and recommended highly by Fulbright, but he also had to win over committees of Rhodes interviewers in Little Rock and New Orleans. Clinton impressed the committees with his knowledge of world affairs. He breezed through his interviews in Little Rock, and then left for New Orleans. On his way, he stopped in the airport and bought a copy of *Time* magazine to read on the plane. The cover story of the magazine that week reported news of the world's first heart transplant, which in 1968 was regarded as radical surgery. When Bill Clinton arrived in New Orleans one of the things the Rhodes interviewers quizzed him about was heart transplants. Clinton was able to handle the questions easily, thanks to the knowledge he had gained just hours before simply by reading a magazine story.

When Clinton learned he had been selected as a Rhodes scholar, he immediately called his mother. Getting Virginia on the phone, he said, "Well, mother, how do you think I'll look in English tweeds?"

Clinton spent two years at Oxford. He studied international politics, philosophy, and economics, concentrating on study of the Soviet Union, then one of the world's superpowers. Away from the classroom, Clinton loved to dawdle after meals in the school cafeteria, engaging in dialogues with other students. Fellow Rhodes scholar Doug Eakely recalled that the younger English students "were in constant fascination with Bill and he with them. They were so verbally facile. It was expected that you would not just eat and run but eat and talk and debate the great issues of the day until you were thrown out of the dining hall. Bill was always in the thick of it."

In 1969, while still studying in England, Bill received his U.S. military draft notice. After much thought, he decided to make himself available for the draft. He was found to be qualified to serve and was placed in the draft lottery. On December 1, 1969, Clinton received his lottery number, which was high enough to assure that he would never be called into service.

Clinton returned to America in 1970 and enrolled in the law school of Yale University. In the United States, law school has often been an important stop on the path followed by many political leaders as they prepare to become lawmakers. Clinton may have gone to Yale to study for the bar examination, but what he mostly practiced at the school was politics. Immediately after stepping onto the campus in New Haven, Connecticut, Clinton signed up to work for a U.S. Senate candidate named Joe Duffey. Duffey and his aides recognized a born political organizer when they saw one, and Clinton was soon assigned the task of running the campaign in the city of New Haven as well as its suburbs. Clinton worked hard in the campaign, rising early in the morning to round up volunteers, distribute campaign literature in neighborhoods, produce mailings, and step in for Duffey at candidates' events whenever he had to. He slept little and ate on the run.

Duffey finished a distant second in the race, but to Clinton the campaign was hardly a waste of time. Although it turned out to be a losing effort, he gained valuable experience. Clinton was certain that after earning his law degree, he would return to Arkansas to run for public office himself.

After law school, Bill returned to Arkansas where he found a college teaching job while he planned his first political campaign. He failed in that campaign—a race for Congress—but in 1976 won the position of state attorney general. Two years later he won his first term as governor. He served two years but was defeated in the 1980 gubernatorial election. He was reelected governor in 1982 and served four more consecutive terms.

During the 1980s, his leadership and success in governing Arkansas came to the attention of national Democratic Party leaders. In 1992, Bill Clinton won his party's nomination for president, then defeated President George Bush in the fall campaign.

As president, Clinton led his country through a period of tremendous economic growth. Few people were out of work during his administration. Clinton also signed trade agreements with Mexico and Canada and new laws to crack down on crime and control handguns. His wife, Hillary Rodham Clinton, whom he had met at Yale and married in 1975, became a popular though controversial first lady. After the Clintons left the White House Hillary Clinton won election to the U.S. Senate representing New York, becoming the first former first lady in history to be elected to a major political office.

Bill Clinton's administration was also marked by scandal. He was only the second president in U.S. history to be impeached. Members of Congress believed he had lied when asked questions under oath about his romantic relationship with a young woman who worked in the White House. Clinton denied the relationship, but later admitted that it had occurred. Opinion polls reported that a majority of American people believed he was doing a good job as president. Ultimately, the Senate was unable to find the votes to remove him from office, and he finished his presidency and left the White House in January 2001.

"If you live long enough, you'll make mistakes," Bill Clinton once said. "But if you learn from them, you'll be a better person. It's how you handle adversity, not how it affects you. The main thing is never quit, never quit, never quit."

—Hal Marcovitz

George W. Bush

Chapter Forty-two

The Second Gulf War, launched by the United States in the face of strident opposition by some of America's oldest allies, again brought into sharp focus the acuity of George W. Bush. Throughout the 2000 election campaign puzzlement regarding Bush's capacity to serve as the single most powerful man in the world had persisted, continuing into his first year in the White House. His brash Texas folksiness, inexperience with (and seeming indifference to) world affairs, and a regular tendency to mangle the English language were all recurring themes in the early months of his presidency.

This shadow disappeared in the immediate aftermath of the national tragedy on September 11, 2001. The president rose to meet America's greatest crisis since Pearl Harbor, immediately commanding respect and support at home and abroad. For the next two years his Gallup approval rating remained high—even as the stock market lost 20 percent of its value and confidence in the economy went into sharp decline. While protestors around the world demonized the president for invading Iraq, within the United States he managed to preserve a strong political base by projecting a confident leadership style, one that seems to reflect unflinching ability to transform world affairs. Thus the paradox of a notable public figure often viewed as a casually educated and mostly inexperienced lightweight who has embarked on the most ambitious foreign policy crusade since Woodrow Wilson set out after World War I to remake the world in America's image.

In *Bush at War*, Bob Woodward relates a rare but telling piece of presidential introspection. Bush mused to the author about taking command of his national security team in the immediate aftermath of September 11. "If I have any genius or smarts," he told Woodward, "it's the ability to recognize talent, ask them to serve and work with them as a team." Missing from the quotation but implicit in it is the message that the "team" would follow a determined leader filled with a mission and devoid of self-doubt.

Whatever lethargy may have once possessed him, Bush immediately found resolve as wartime commander in chief. While only the unfolding of tumultuous events and the sharp judgment of historical perspective will determine the relative

George W. Bush is part of a distinguished American political family. His paternal grandfather, Prescott Bush, was a U.S. senator from Connecticut from 1952 to 1962, and his father, George H. W. Bush, served as the forty-first president of the United States from 1989 to 1993. George W. is the second president to be the son of a president— John and John Quincy Adams being the first father and son to have each achieved the nation's highest political office.

George W. Bush graduated from Phillips Academy, Andover, in 1964. He received his BA in History from Yale University in 1968 and his MBA from the Harvard Business School in 1975.

George W. Bush with his father George H. W. Bush and his mother Barbara Bush. Young George was nine years old when this photo was taken in the summer of 1955.

wisdom or folly of Bush's international venture, one principal aspect of it is already unmistakably clear. However much he is coached by significant others, the new American worldview is that of George W. Bush.

Once the conventional wisdom concerning Bush's major aides—Dick Cheney, Donald Rumsfeld, Colin Powell, and Condoleezza Rice, along with Paul Wolfowitz and Richard Perle—held that the inexperienced president needed heavyweights to tell him what to think, what to do, and how to do it. As events after September 11 now clearly indicate, however, they function less as advisors and more as managers of this president's ideas. Tactics and strategy are surely open for discussion. But general objectives and Bush's fixed determination to achieve them are not. Perhaps the strongest impression left by *Bush at War* is of the president's command style. Unlike John F. Kennedy in the Cuban Missile Crisis or Lyndon B. Johnson in the Vietnam War, Bush did not seek advice, options, or multiple scenarios. He issued orders. Perhaps this decisive clarity is instinctively transmitted to popular opinion. It certainly stands at variance with earlier perceptions of the man.

One legitimate question for debate is the source of his self-confidence. Primary is the influence of the Bush Dynasty, now in its fifth generation of permanent power but only dimly appreciated as an experience that provided all the training necessary to live life and play a dominant role in the affairs of the nation. The comparison between Bush's formal and informal education is revealing. It is often remarked that George W. Bush, afforded the best educational opportunities available in the United States, responded by insisting upon intellectual mediocrity. In fact, Bush's three academic experiences are almost insignificant in his "education." A study of President Bush's education must be rooted more in family training and experience than in prep school, college, or university. In the fullest sense, young Bush brought to his elite educational experience a value system fully forged in the wild oil frontier of West Texas and the upper-class haunts of the children of Houston's business aristocracy.

His formal education began prosaically enough at Sam Houston Elementary School in Midland, Texas. After the family moved to Houston in 1959, the young man was enrolled at the Kinkaid School, a private and exclusive redoubt for the children of Houston's petrobusiness elite. Two years later, deferring to his parents' wishes at the age of fifteen, he went off far away to Andover, Massachusetts, to Phillips Academy.

For most of American history Phillips Academy, or just "Andover" (the names are used interchangeably), twenty miles north of Boston, has been steeped in the traditions of the upper class. A daunting legacy hovered over the legendary campus, the nation's oldest boarding school. Its hundred-odd buildings have been inhabited by generations of graduates whose success touched every corner of American life. In 1960 it remained a refuge for the boys of the American elites, entrance based largely if not exclusively on family prominence, connections and, as with the Bushes, lineage. His father, graduated nineteen years earlier, had been named, in then-familiar parlance, "Best All Around Fellow" in his class.

"He was one of the cool guys…. He rose to a certain prominence for no ostensible, visible reason…. Obviously, he inherited some extraordinary political skills."

The academic and social structure of Phillips Academy resonated with eternal verities, discipline, particularly punctuality, religiosity, and continuous academic and sports activity. The roughhousing atmosphere of the playing fields and residence halls reflected the kind of muscular Christianity favored by Theodore Roosevelt for the young men of the American elite. Young Bush, not blessed with the athletic skills of his father, more than compensated socially. He did try baseball, gave rock music a whirl, and became head cheerleader. Arguably the most popular boy due to his exuberant infectious personality, Bush drew into his circle peers who did excel at sports and scholarship. They became his admirers and friends, some on a lifelong basis. More importantly, young Bush began to exhibit at Andover characteristics that would mark his maturity as a politician.

In an interview with Bill Minutaglio for *First Son: George W. Bush and the Bush Family Dynasty* (1999), an Andover schoolmate tried to describe the essence of the teenaged George W. Bush. "George was always part of a small group of seven or eight guys who were really, well, you have to call them the big men on campus. He was one of the cool guys…. He rose to a certain prominence for no ostensible, visible reason…. Obviously, he inherited some extraordinary political skills."

Bush would need them. Northeastern winters lasted forever for the young Texan. Inside the classrooms, moreover, he perceived the academic sophistication of his peers as an obstacle course that he had no particular interest in testing. Instead he concentrated on being mischievous, the leading boy prankster whose peers admired his nerve in testing the limits of order and pomposity. "I'm sure he took some things seriously," another classmate recalled, "but he was more interested in social standing than what grades he had in order to get into Yale." Bush and his friends "would walk around with a certain confidence, bravado, a little swagger," Minutaglio wrote in *First Son.* As head cheerleader the swagger took center stage. As "High Commissioner" of an informal but elaborately organized stickball league, young Bush presided with mock solemnity as judge and jury in mediating the endless arguments that competitive boys have in their games. Mock solemnity, wigs, disguises, top hats, and pranks. As another classmate recalls for Bill Minutaglio, "It's very hard to get below the surface of George, he is so facile and so personable…. He was already who he was, but being at Andover gave him a chance to hone his skills."

In June 1964 George W. Bush graduated from Andover and returned to Texas to begin his real education, just at the moment when the Bush Dynasty's torch was passed to his father. In Connecticut, Senator Prescott Bush announced his retirement at about the same time that, in Houston, George H. W. Bush sought to replace him in the upper

George W. Bush's 1968 senior class photograph, and the title page from *The Old Campus*. The 1968 Yale class was the last for an all-male student body.

During George W.'s four years at Yale, his father was involved in political campaigns that attracted national publicity. In 1964, the senior Bush ran unsuccessfully for the United States Senate from Texas and two years later he was elected to the House of Representatives. George W. was involved in each campaign.

THE OLD CAMPUS
1968

A YALE BANNER PUBLICATION

chamber. Thus the recent Andover graduate, on his way to Yale, returned home to join his father's campaign for the United States Senate. At eighteen, his real education began.

Although Republican John Tower had won a special Senate election in 1961, serious Republican candidates were still strange characters across an endless Texas landscape filled with habitual Democrats. This was particularly so in 1964, when the almost manic campaign of President Lyndon Baines Johnson dominated both state and national political attention. In Texas, with the president claiming possession of nearly all of the political spectrum, George H. W. Bush ran toward the right-wing fringes, opposing civil rights, nuclear test ban negotiations with the Soviet Union, foreign aid, anti-poverty initiatives, and Martin Luther King Jr. Beyond political issues, however, Bush faced the even more daunting hurdle of his manner and lineage.

With his son alongside, Bush exerted great effort in a flawed attempt to disguise his gentlemanly manner and northeastern bearing. Traveling in a bus caravan dubbed "The Bandwagon for Bush," he gamely listened at stop after stop to the Black Mountain Boys working up a country and western performance, accompanied by a chorus of Republican women, the "Bush Bluebonnet Belles," offering such rustic verse as "Oh, the sun's gonna shine in the Senate someday! George Bush is going to chase them liberals away!"

Amidst the rhetorical hokum, George Bush seemed inauthentic. Never convincing in western garb, he remained in the mind's eye in blue blazer and rep tie, reflecting the country club gentility of his Greenwich, Andover, and Yale roots, the picture of a well-bred Yankee aristocrat created over generations of wealth and political influence. He embodied the great dynasty that Bushes and Walkers represent. (However strenuously the family continues to deny the "dynasty" appellation, there is no other term for the century-long melding of privilege and power routinely exercised by the Bush and Walker families.)

In the Gilded Age of the last three decades of the nineteenth century the modern American industrial and commercial aristocracy took its form as a permanent elite, insuring succeeding generations access to wealth and its rewards, including political power. Samuel Prescott Bush (1863–1948), great grandfather to President George W. Bush, was born in New York but became a steel and railroad baron in Columbus, Ohio. His impressive dossier includes serving as the first president of the National Association of Manufacturers, then as now the nation's most powerful industrial lobby. Also a founding member of the United States Chamber of Commerce and a Federal Reserve director, Samuel P. Bush became an adviser to President Herbert Hoover and a member of his administration. Noted for his prominent role in civic associations, Bush, a varsity athlete in football and baseball, also helped establish the sport of football at Ohio State University.

Samuel's son Prescott, father to a president and grandfather to another, added great luster to the family's standing. Born in 1895 to wealth and status, he was properly educated in prep school, on to Yale, varsity baseball and football, nationally known golfer, Skull & Bones, World War I combat as a field artillery captain in front-line service in France, before careers on Wall Street and in the United States Senate.

In 1921, Prescott Bush married Dorothy Walker, from another powerful family of merchants and bankers. Her grandfather, David Douglas Walker, made a fortune in dry goods and rose to prominence in civic affairs in St. Louis. Dorothy's father, George Herbert Walker, a founding partner of Wall Street's oldest and most powerful private investment house, Brown Brothers Harriman, became a confidante of Franklin Delano Roosevelt. The congenialities shared by the Bush-Walker family included golf, the favored sporting indulgence of the elite in those generations. Prescott Bush achieved international recognition as an amateur champion. His wife's father, the Wall Street banker, gave the family name to the Walker Cup competition between American and British teams.

The essence of the family's story over the past half-century is the move from the New England patrician class to the hard-knuckle cultural bramble of Texas. Remarkably resilient and successful in building an oil fortune in the havoc of the West Texas oil patch, George H. W. Bush moved the family base to Houston, capital city of the American petrochemical industry, solidified his class and caste base in the opulent suburbs, and watched his family grow under the discipline of the redoubtable Barbara Walker Bush. In 1964, in running for the Senate, Bush sought to emulate his ancestors and in-laws, observed every day by his eldest son.

The impact of family dynamics in the socialization of the forty-third president cannot be overestimated. For ten years after his sixth birthday, young George watched his two principal role models with great intensity. His grandfather, elected to the Senate in 1952, periodically arrived in Midland, a commanding Yankee patrician visiting the family's outpost on the oil derrick frontier. Also during these years, Poppy began his own strenuous efforts to build a political profile of his own. A relentless civic man, involved in his church, service clubs, and philanthropic campaigns, George H. W. Bush genuinely liked his peers, the rising class of accomplished men who wrenched fortunes out of the petroleum landscape. Moving among them with his loopy smile, mouth slightly agape, exchanging a joke or a confidence, shaking all hands, purring the small talk that is coin of the realm for politicians, George H. W. Bush became a natural aristocrat on this untamed society. There are few less likely sites for a Yale Club than Midland, Texas, but there it was, with dinner dances and strenuous tennis matches, filling up with rising men compatible with Bush values. Here became an incubus for the Republican Party in Texas, which would send Bush forward to vie for a Senate seat in 1964.

Because the summer vacation of 1964 ended before the election campaign, George W. headed for New Haven to follow family tradition at Yale. After settling in briefly, the young man returned to Houston for the final hours of the election. His father, crushed by over 300,000 votes by the incumbent Democrat, Senator Ralph Yarborough, reacted with typical aplomb. He empathized with the feelings of disappointed family and friends, and avoided bitterness toward political adversaries who had defeated him through a campaign marked by caricature and crude innuendo. Bush the war hero and successful oilman disappeared into the caricature of an outsider, an interloper sent by shadowy intriguers to somehow hoodwink Texans. Provincialism triumphed, and an observant son carefully noted it. There would never be a question of the son's authenticity as a Texan.

Back at Yale, Bush would confront a daunting legacy. His grandfather had at Yale been a scholar, varsity athlete in football and baseball, championship-caliber golfer, member of the famed "Whiffenpoof" singers, and served on the Yale board. His father had, if anything, done even more at Yale as student, baseball captain, and as a kind of peer-respected student statesman. George W., naturally assuming that his generation of Yalies would be similarly commissioned to service and status, found instead frustration bordering on bitterness. During his freshman year, in the direct aftermath of his father's political defeat, young Bush had an encounter that would permanently sour his feelings toward Yale.

This most galling event came about in a chance meeting on campus—when Bush introduced himself to Yale's famously controversial university chaplain, William Sloane Coffin, a nationally prominent antiwar activist. As a Yale senior in 1948, Coffin had been "tapped" for the secret Skull and Bones Society by its leader, George H. W. Bush. A generation later, in the wake of the elder Bush's crushing political defeat at the hands of Senator Yarborough, Coffin said to the younger Bush, "Oh, yes, I know your father. Frankly, he was beaten by a better man." This moment provided a kind of negative epiphany for the young man from Texas. Resolutely positioning himself outside of Yale's turbulent Sixties mainstream, Bush chose the safety of a fraternity culture increasingly marginalized and trivialized by most of his peers.

Much of the consternation he felt as an undergraduate grew out of the counterculture that invaded American campuses both great and modest. Elevated for the first time in American colleges and universities were the values inimical to established traditions of family, country, and noblesse oblige embraced by his forebears. Public figures like his father and grandfather were routinely excoriated as standard-bearers of a society whose primary institutions and policies were found by increasingly radicalized students as not only deficient but positively malevolent.

Teach-ins, sit-ins, street demonstrators, challenges to professors and college administrators, alliances with populist fringe groups, Marxist and Freudian analyses of self and society—all struck young Bush as shockingly wrongheaded. Traditionalists at Yale and elsewhere did attempt to counter the radicalization of campus life, including many Republican and conservative student groups, but Bush remained resolutely apolitical. He retreated into the safety of fraternity life, with its ubiquitous social activities featuring alcohol, parties, intramural sports, pursuit of young women, and assorted weekend adventures.

It was a comfortable routine of intramural sports and fraternity fun. His style became centered on the Delta Kappa Epsilon fraternity, the legendary DKE, the quintessential fun-and-games refuge for athletes and the descendants of Yale's elite. His father, perhaps naturally, had been chapter president, a position that George W. succeeded to for his senior year.

The recollections of his fraternity brothers are filled with nostalgic warmth for the chapter president who made it to the White House. Obviously, and despite the vastly different proportions, George W. Bush's young undergraduate peers recognized and followed certain personality traits that a dubious national political world would come to accept only haltingly a generation later. "He's the great sun around which a universe revolved," a DKE told Bill Minutaglio. "He radiated star quality, but never in an unapproachable way."

Over the following four years the young Texan made lifelong friends—and a few detractors as well. In the latter category, one would prove a continuing nemesis. Gary Trudeau, author of the syndicated and widely read cartoon series "Doonesbury," knew Bush casually at Yale when the Texan served as DKE rush chairman. Years later, Trudeau would sardonically tell Ted Koppel on *Nightline* that when it came to deciding how many kegs of beer for a party, "I have to say, George Bush showed great leadership qualities during those meetings." Trudeau routinely mocks President Bush as an invisible person beneath a ten-gallon hat spouting inanities. The continuing ridicule of Bush, certainly less pervasive as his accomplishments have produced great popular approval, is nonetheless rooted in the modest biography he brought to the White House. In large part, the arrogant anti-intellectualism of his career at Yale continued to resonate.

Even the prize of the DKE presidency, a trophy in his father's time, became devalued in the fevered political context of the Sixties. The once-mighty sway of the so-called Greek System of fraternity and secret society membership atrophied to become the fodder for condescension. Ensconced in this narrowing world of fun and foolishness, with academic responsibilities casually tolerated, George W. Bush and his like-minded associates spent the mid-Sixties pleasantly enough.

The focus of his senior year centered on the "tapping" of Bush for the ultra-secret elite society, Skull and Bones. Formed at Yale in 1832 out of a recondite hodgepodge of Germanic mysticism, it pledged generations of members to absolute secrecy. In its campus "tomb" on High Street, a two-story house with lounges, library, dining room, and an "inner temple," the selected handful of that year's seniors came into contact with Bonesmen of old, collectively the generations of the elite from Wall Street, corporate America, Washington, and world capitals. Alexandra Robbins's *Secrets of the Tomb* (2002) recounts the extraordinary list of famous and powerful Americans tapped for Skull and Bones—a litany of the aristocracy, including family dynasties named Bundy, Harriman, Lord, Rockefeller, Taft, and Whitney, as well as the Bushes. Revered by the members and derided by critics, Yale's secret societies enclosed young men in a self-congratulatory world in which the insiders found much of college's values, even as they misbehaved. George W. Bush's minor scrapes with the police, commonplace enough among fraternity carousers of that era, would later provide fodder for tall tales of youthful indiscretion. He did not much like Yale even as he grew more self-confident.

His alienation from Yale's purported snobbishness, its "heavy" intellectualism, its estrangement from loyalty, tradition, and the purported commonsensical mind of the American electorate, served to reinforce Bush's commitment to tradition. He

DELTA KAPPA EPSILON

FOUNDED 1844

DKE

Class of 1968
R. H. Allen, Robert E.L. Beebe, Daniel M. Begel, D. Bergman, Roland W. Betts, George W. Bush, C.E. Thomas Clevland, Edgar M. Cullman, Millard D. Davidson, David W. Davis, Robert J. Dieter, John R. Emmons, Donald B. Ersenat, James D. Fisher, Steven L. Freidman, G. Gregory Gallico, Matthew T. Gay, B. Heeseler, Robert T. Hume, Clay Johnson, Collister Johnson, Paul B. Jones, Robert J. Keuh, D. Knuth-Winterfeldt, Donald W. Koerlin, Kenneth R. Kurtz, Franklin H. Levy, James B. Lockhart, Peter F. Markle, Samuel Martin, Stephen W. Mayberg, Frederick V. Mc-Carthy, Allan McDowell, Livy Miller, David R. Patterson, Joseph E. Potter, Clark T. Randt, Robert A. Reisner, Steven R. Rummel, John T. Sartore, Robert T. Savage, William H. Sawyer, Donald A. Schollander, Kenneth B. Schulman, Steven M. Shapiro, J. Courtney Shevelson, Chris C. Taylor, Robert J. Ternes, D. Townsend, Paul Tully, Joseph T. Ward, William B. Wemple, Kenneth E. White, Ronald F. Whitney, Geoffrey R.H. Woglom.

Class of 1969
Robert E. Arras, John B. Babcock, Charles W. Banta, Francis A. Boyer, Timothy P. Briney, Richard D. Bruns, H. Douglas Connell, Walter J. Cummings, David M. Daest, Bardfute W. Davenport, Mark B. Dayton, Steven Dixon, Brian J. Dowling, William Evans, Jerry DuV. Gary, J. P. Goldsmith, Timothy Harris, David Heckler, John M. Hemingway, Calvin Hill, Robert G. Hoban, J. William Howerton, John M. Keeling, Merritt B. Kleber, Phillip M. Laugh-lin, Robert E. Levin, Frederick Livingston, Richard E. Lassen, William McKenna, John E. Mackey, Walter A. Marting, Kimball H. Morsman, B. Owens, William A. Palmer, Charles S. Peck, Daniel B. Rothstein, Ralph S. Sando, Jonathan Stern, Duane A. Selander, Robert J. Sokolowski, Karl A. Spangenberg, Frank J. Sprole, Gregory N. Thomas, Daniel M. Tucker, John B. Waldman, A. Welles, Michael M. Wood, Scott A. Williams, James N. Worcestor.

Class of 1970
Gerard D. Cameron, Gordon H. Clark, Glenn E. DeChabert, Wayne H. Ewing, Harvey F. Gerber, William A. Harper, Charles B. Hogan, Gerard B. Hughes, Terrence J. Jackson, Stephen C. Jones, William B. Katz, Bradford A. Lee, Joseph D. Messinger, Van Midgrly, Samuel R. Miller, George Noble, Jeff D. Palmer, Robert Potts, Peter A. Radice, William R. Seelbach, William H. Starbuck, James B. Stryker, Edgar L. Taplin, John C. Train, Chris Trower, Todd Wheeler, Richard C. Whittlesey, Edward M. Wright, Jeff Almquist, Woody Britton, Wayne Cutler, Larry Dautch, James Dempsey, Pete D'Chellis, Tony Gaslevich, Charles Stewart.

256

DELTA KAPPA EPSILON
FOUNDED 1844

George W. Bush attended Yale from 1964 to 1968 (this photograph was taken in 1965). He was the fourth generation to do so.

Bush was elected president of the Delta Kappa Epsilon fraternity—his father's former fraternity. (His name appears in the second line under "Class of 1968"; the DKE house is pictured on the right.) Bush was also "tapped" for membership in Skull and Bones, his father and grandfather's club. Almost all who knew Bush as a fellow student have described his charismatic and exuberant personality.

left New Haven with no doubts that he, like his father and grandfather before him, represented that older, wiser American polity. He would eventually pursue these values not as a New England Yankee Ivy Leaguer, but as its stylistic opposite.

Embedded in this family socialization is religiosity, a force that has gathered momentum in recent years in defining and shaping President Bush's view of himself and his domestic and foreign policies.

His family insists that social class does not matter while all the time seeing the world through the natural assumptions of who should prevail, i.e., achievement through family lineage, association with similar others, respect for economic accomplishment, and use of government to promote and protect this ethic which allows success on the highest levels with a value system determined by the simple ethos of market capitalism.

Attracted by the practicalities of the bottom line, Bush has learned to dismiss those abstractions that challenge it. As president, he professes to see no hypocrisy between his own admission to elite schools based on moderate academic qualifications and his opposition to Michigan's preferential formula according weight to race. He asked the Supreme Court to rule the Michigan system unconstitutional, noting that "African-American students and some Hispanic students and Native American students receive 20 points out of a maximum of 150, not because of any academic achievement or life experience, but solely because they are African-American, Hispanic or Native American." Family legacy, yes. Skin color counterbalancing racism, no. It would be difficult to explore this contradiction, and so he ignores it, confident that his family's traditions are sufficient. His SAT scores (566 verbal, 640 math) were no obstacle to elite matriculation in the system that prevailed then and now, for the children of alumni, particularly rich and influential alumni.

Another "practical" tenet of family faith is revealed religion, although the style and content of religious practice has changed substantially over the Bush generations. In its March 10, 2003, cover story, *Newsweek* explored the role of religion in defining the most controversial aspects of the Bush presidency. The account traces the family's religious bent over the years down to the establishmentarian Episcopalian traditions when they lived in Yankee Connecticut. The move to Texas gradually led to an opening to the religious right, fundamentalist, evangelical, born-again Christianity that became such a potent force in the Republican Party's capture of power in the South in the 1980s. As George W. assumed a surrogate's power in his father's political rise, the firmest vase lay on the religious right, where the son found a spiritual home in mid-life. He has often cited biblical study and the personalized relationship with the Deity for his rescue from excessive drinking. As a friend put it, "Good-bye Jack Daniels, hello Jesus." As Bush observed to a clergymen's group, "There is only one reason that I am in the Oval Office and not in a bar. I found faith. I found God. I am here because of the power of prayer."

All American presidents are required, as a matter of political necessity, to pay some level of obeisance to religious observance, of course. For the forty-third president, however, religion is revealed and fundamental, not intellectual and abstract. The veteran Washington journalist Elizabeth Drew referred to his "messianic streak." The far side of George W.'s "aw shucks" regular guy persona is his sense of destiny: if something is big enough and important enough, he believes it is his destiny to right it. As his formal educational experiences taught him to suspect rationality and intellectualism, space opened for his personal religious experience.

By the time of his 1968 graduation, Bush's father had been elected to Congress from a Houston district, and in 1970 again lost an attempt at a Senate seat before winning nomination as U.S. ambassador to the United Nations. George W.'s resume proved much more modest. He returned home and entered into the much-debated process through which he avoided active duty in the Vietnam War by securing a much-coveted Texas Air National Guard commission. With the sons of other prominent Lone Star State families, he spent parts of the next years flying jet planes safely away from the murderous conflict in Southeast Asia. Settling into a relaxed bachelor lifestyle with similarly inclined young people, he tended to re-create his Yale lifestyle while slowly pondering the future. Unsatisfying jobs and low-level dabbling in Republican politics followed, and five years passed.

In 1973, Bush and eight hundred others began in the MBA program at Harvard Business School. The prestige of this degree rested largely on its alumni, whose careers in the United States and around the world constituted an interlocked system of power and influence. The pedagogy rested on case studies, specific examples of situations relying on facts to be analyzed and policy options to be taken. For the first time, the twenty-seven-year-old Bush took with great interest to a kind of formal education. Avoiding grand theorizing, social policy, and abstruse academic subjects, Bush fully and successfully took on the curriculum and interacted positively with his like-minded classmates. Nonetheless, the unstable world of the Nixon presidency dominated the climate within which the business school stood isolated in its commitment to entrepreneurial capitalism.

Bush again resolutely shunned campus turmoil, and concluded that Harvard, like Yale, had little to teach him about his own value system. After two years, he headed straight for the life his father had trail blazed a generation earlier: the wild oil fields. George W. Bush returned to his childhood home, Midland, Texas.

Formal education had ended. In sum, he more or less despised Phillips Academy, Yale and Harvard; each in its own way the antithesis of the values lived and learned by the family in Texas. Years later, during his father's 1992 reelection campaign, according to Minutaglio's *First Son*, George W. fulminated about "of what he hated about the cynics in the northeastern media, all those guilt-laden intellectuals who had everything in common with the arrogant, suffocating products of Yale and Harvard."

As a boy and young man during time spent in Andover, New Haven, and Cambridge, Bush insulated himself from the dominant campus ethos, successfully

In 1968, George W. Bush joined the Texas Air National Guard. He served as a F-102 fighter pilot. When the commanding officer of the unit asked him, "Why do you want to join?" Bush replied, "I want to be a fighter pilot because my father was." George H. W. Bush had been the youngest commissioned officer in the U.S. Navy during World War II.

"There is only one reason that I am in the Oval Office and not in a bar. I found faith. I found God. I am here because of the power of prayer."

shutting out "the Sixties" which howled about him preaching values and habits repugnant to his family tradition. The worldview that has come to mark his presidency is largely shaped by those years. Scion of a generations-old dynasty of wealth and power, George W. Bush's nature and nurture comprised the only education he would ever need.

The process of linking the biographical elements in the career of a public person is certainly an inexact art form. Aspects of George W. Bush's public persona seem to have discernible roots, however. Never comfortable with the easy pragmatism and relativism so common among political people, he has always implicitly trusted people who meet the definition of character worked out by the Bush Dynasty.

As president, he appointed as his principal officers men whose fervently held beliefs matched his own. Sure of themselves to the point of dogmatism, Cheney, Rumsfeld, Wolfowitz and their outriders were brought into positions of high power not to advise President George W. Bush so much as to carry out their vision by a president who believed in it as strongly as they did themselves. Rooted in a clear sense of righteousness, a businessman's notion of common sense, with the marketplace the judge of value and reward, fundamental religious verities and the clear superiority of American institutions, the Bush administration would pursue a breathtaking restructure of U.S. domestic and foreign policy.

At home, no president since the ill-fated Herbert Hoover had trusted his fortunes so much to the foibles of supply-side economics, where fiscal and monetary policy concentrating on tax cuts benefiting the privileged and powerful would pass down through society to increase the general welfare. Abroad, the export of U.S. democratic institutions to areas of the globe and cultural traditions with no experience with it (or apparent taste for it) constituted an idealism that harkened back eight decades to Woodrow Wilson's failed plans to "make the world safe for democracy."

From the vantage point of the spring of 2003, therefore, the pending question concerns not at all the willingness of Bush to attempt a historic shift in global balance of power. Rather it is the wisdom of that vision. Unlike all his predecessors stretching back to Roosevelt and Truman, Bush seems almost anxious to give up the multilateral framework within which the United States clearly played the role of leader of alliance systems. Upon the wisdom of unilateralism Bush has staked his reputation and most likely his presidency. He remains remarkably self-assured in knowing what he knows. Otherwise, he shows little curiosity. In sum, an irregular education.

—J. F. Watts

A Selective Guide to Presidential Biographies

This listing is a sampling of the biographies available dealing with the lives of the presidents of the United States. Many of these titles have been reprinted; the date listed is that of the original publication. The bibliographies and footnotes in each of the following books should be useful for further study. This bibliography is based upon Tom Trescott and Dan Weinberg, "The Essential Presidential Book Shelf: A Selective Readers' and Collectors' Guide," *The Rail Splitter*, vol. 7 no. 4 (Spring 2002).

George Washington (Federalist, 1789–1797)

James Thomas Flexner's *George Washington* (four vols., 1965–1972) is thoroughly researched and well written. Essential for studying the life of the first president.

Douglas Southall Freeman's *George Washington: A Biography* (seven vols., 1948–1957) is a distinguished work by an eminent historian. Volumes one and two deal with Washington's early life. This is the definitive portrait of Washington.

George Washington: The Man Behind the Myths (1999), by William Rasmussen and Robert Tilton, is an outstanding combination of narrative, analysis, and visual imagery. The authors give an original analysis of Washington's public and private lives.

John Adams (Federalist, 1797–1801)

Page Smith's *John Adams* (two vols., 1962) was the first major biography of Adams completed after the publication of the Adams Papers. First rate.

John Adams: A Life (1992), by John Ferling, is an excellent one-volume work.

David McCullough's *John Adams* (2001) is a popular and well-written biography by a Pulitzer Prize winner.

Thomas Jefferson (Democratic-Republican, 1801–1809)

Dumas Malone's *Jefferson and His Times* (six vols., 1948–1981) is one of the greatest contributions to American historical literature in the twentieth century. Volume one, *Jefferson the Virginian* (1948), deals with young Jefferson.

Thomas Jefferson and the New Nation: A Biography (1970), by Merrill Peterson, is perhaps the best one-volume life of the third president.

James Madison (Democratic-Republican, 1809–1817)

Irving Brant's *James Madison* (6 vols., 1941–1961) is the definitive work on Madison. Brant's *The Fourth President: A Life of James Madison* (1970) is a masterful condensation of the multi-volume original.

James Madison: A Biography (1971), by Robert Ketcham, is a well-written review of Madison's life.

James Monroe (Democratic-Republican, 1817–1825)

Harry Ammon's *James Monroe* (1971) is a good survey of Monroe's life.

William Cresson's *James Monroe* (1946) is a scholarly biography of Monroe.

John Quincy Adams (Democratic-Republican, 1825–1829)

John Quincy Adams (1972), by Marie Hecht, is a good survey of Adams' life.

Lynn Parsons's *John Quincy Adams* (1998) is a well-written recent biography.

Andrew Jackson (Democrat, 1829–1837)

The definitive biography of Jackson is Robert Remini's three-volume *Andrew Jackson* (1977–1984). Volume one, *Andrew Jackson and the Course of American Empire, 1767–1821* (1977), covers Jackson's early life.

Marquis James's *Andrew Jackson* (two vols., 1933–1937) was considered the standard life of Jackson until the Remini study.

Martin Van Buren (Democrat, 1837–1841)

Denis Lynch's *An Epoch and a Man: Martin Van Buren and His Times* (1929) is the best available biography of Van Buren.

John Niven's *Martin Van Buren and the Romantic Age of American Politics* (1983) is the first modern biography of Van Buren based extensively on his personal papers.

William Henry Harrison (Whig, 1841)

Old Tippecanoe: William Henry Harrison and His Times (1939), a sympathetic biography by Freeman Cleaves, is an excellent survey of Harrison's early life.

Dorothy Goebel's *William Henry Harrison* (1926) remains essential to the study of Harrison. Goebel also wrote the excellent article on Harrison for the *Dictionary of American Biography*, volume eight.

John Tyler (Whig, 1841–1845)

Oliver Chitwood's *John Tyler: Champion of the Old South* (1939) is a scholarly work on a complex personality, the first of the accidental presidents.

The essential book on Tyler is Robert Seager's *And Tyler Too: A Biography of John and Julia Tyler* (1963).

James K. Polk (Democrat, 1845–1849)

Eugene McCormac's *James K. Polk* (1922) is an excellent account of the first "dark horse" in a presidential race.

Charles Sellers's *James K. Polk* (two vols., 1957–1966) is a carefully researched study.

Zachary Taylor (Whig, 1849–1850)

K. Jack Bauer's *Zachary Taylor: Soldier, Planter, Statesman of the Old Southwest* (1985) is a balanced and thoroughly researched biography of a complex personality.

The definitive life of "Old Rough and Ready" is Holman Hamilton's two-volume Zachary Taylor (1941–1951).

Millard Fillmore (Whig, 1850–1853)

Millard Fillmore: Biography of a President (1959), by Robert Rayback, is a good biography of an underrated president.

Franklin Pierce (Democrat, 1853–1857)

Franklin Pierce: Young Hickory of the Granite Hills (1931; revised 1958), by Roy Nichols, is a discerning portrait of Pierce, and the only scholarly biography of the man. Nichols expanded his research on Pierce with a series of articles that appeared in numerous journals.

James Buchanan (Democrat, 1857–1861)

Philip Klein's *President James Buchanan: A Biography* (1962) is a scholarly biography of one of the most misunderstood chief executives.

Abraham Lincoln (Republican, 1861–1865)

David Donald's outstanding 1995 biography *Lincoln* won the Pulitzer Prize.

The Last Best Hope of Earth: Abraham Lincoln and the Promise of America (1993), by Mark Neely Jr., is an excellent one-volume analysis.

With Malice Toward None: The Life of Abraham Lincoln (1977) by Stephen Oates is another worthwhile study of the sixteenth president.

Carl Sandburg's *Abraham Lincoln* (six vols., 1926–1939) is essential for understanding Lincoln. Sandburg captured the essence of the Lincoln myth and its importance to Americans.

Benjamin Thomas's *Abraham Lincoln: A Biography* (1952) was the classic one-volume life of Lincoln until publication of the Donald study.

Andrew Johnson (Republican-Union, 1865–1869)

Hans Trefousse's *Andrew Johnson: A Biography* (1989) is a full-length biography written by the foremost authority on the Reconstruction period.

Ulysses S. Grant (Republican, 1869–1877)

William McFeely's *Grant: A Biography* (1981) won the Pulitzer Prize.

Ulysses S. Grant: The Triumph over Adversity, 1822–1865 (2000) is the first of two projected volumes by Brooks Simpson.

Jean Smith's *Grant* (2001) is a recent work that is exhaustively researched and wonderfully written.

Rutherford B. Hayes (Republican, 1877–1881)

Harry Barnard's *Rutherford B. Hayes and His America* (1954) is an excellent biography.

Ari Hoogenboom's *Rutherford B. Hayes: Warrior and President* (1996) is a comprehensive biography.

James A. Garfield (Republican, 1881)

The best account of Garfield and the "gilded age" is Allan Peskin's *James Abram Garfield* (1978).

John Taylor's *Garfield of Ohio* (1970) is a fine study of the president who served only six months before he was assassinated.

W. W. Wasson's *James A. Garfield: His Religion and Education* (1952) is a well-documented monograph.

Chester A. Arthur (Republican, 1881–1885)

The only full-length biography of Arthur is Thomas Reeves's *Gentleman Boss: The Life of Chester Alan Arthur* (1975). It is an excellent book.

Grover Cleveland (Democrat, 1885–1889; 1893–1897)

Allan Nevins's *Grover Cleveland* (1932) is the best biography of Cleveland, written by one of the great twentieth-century American historians. Nevins interviewed Cleveland family members and also had access to the president's personal papers.

While Nevins stresses Cleveland's courage, Alyn Brodsky emphasizes his integrity in *Grover Cleveland: A Study in Character* (2000).

Benjamin Harrison (Republican, 1889–1893)

Harry Sievers's *Benjamin Harrison* (three vols., 1952–1968) is the only comprehensive biography. Volume one, *Hoosier Warrior, 1833–1865* (1952) deals with Harrison's education.

William McKinley (Republican, 1897–1901)

Margaret Leech's *In the Days of McKinley* (1959) is an important analysis of McKinley.

H. Wayne Morgan's *William McKinley and His America* (1963) is a masterful study.

Theodore Roosevelt (Republican, 1901–1909)

Power and Responsibility: The Life and Times of Theodore Roosevelt (1961) is an excellent study by William Harbaugh.

David McCullough's superb biography of young TR, *Mornings on Horseback* (1982), won the National Book Award.

Nathan Miller's *Theodore Roosevelt: A Life* (1992) is an excellent one-volume study.

Two volumes by Edmund Morris, *The Rise of Theodore Roosevelt* (1979) and *Theodore Rex* (2001), promise to become the definitive biography.

William Howard Taft (Republican, 1909–1913)

Henry Pringle's *The Life and Times of William Howard Taft* (two vols., 1939) remains the best biography of the only president who also served as chief justice of the Supreme Court.

Woodrow Wilson (Democrat, 1913–1921)

August Heckscher's *Woodrow Wilson* (1991) is the best one-volume study.

Arthur Link's five-volume *Wilson* (1947–1955) is outstanding. Volume one, *The Road to the White House* (1947), deals with Wilson's early years.

Woodrow Wilson (1978), by Arthur Walworth, received the Pulitzer Prize for biography.

Warren G. Harding (Republican, 1921–1923)

Francis Russell's *The Shadow of Blooming Grove: Warren G. Harding and His Times* (1968) is still the best biography of Harding.

Calvin Coolidge (Republican, 1923–1929)

Donald McCoy's *Calvin Coolidge: The Quiet President* (1967) is an objective scholarly biography.

William Allen White's *Puritan in Babylon: The Story of Calvin Coolidge* (1938) is a well-written biography by a famous newspaper editor.

Herbert Hoover (Republican, 1929–1933)

David Burner's *Herbert Hoover* (1979) is a scholarly biography.

George Nash's *The Life of Herbert Hoover* (three vols., 1983–1996) will be the definitive study. It has been subsidized by the Hoover Presidential Library Association. Volume one, *The Engineer, 1874–1914* (1983), covers Hoover's education in great detail.

Franklin D. Roosevelt (Democrat, 1933–1945)

James MacGregor Burns's *Roosevelt* (two vols., 1956–1970) was the first complete biography of Franklin D. Roosevelt. It has maintained its reputation and is still a standard biography of FDR.

FDR: A History (five vols., 1972–2000) is a sweeping chronicle, incomplete due to the death of author Kenneth Davis.

Frank Freidel's *Franklin D. Roosevelt* (four vols., 1952–1973) focuses on Roosevelt's life through the first two years of the New Deal. Volume one is indispensable for understanding FDR's education.

Harry S. Truman (Democrat, 1945–1953)

Robert Ferrell's *Harry S. Truman: A Life* (1994) is a first-rate biography.

A Man of the People: A Life of Harry S. Truman (1995), by Alonzo Hamby, is a scholarly well-written biography.

David McCullough's *Truman* (1992) received the Pulitzer Prize.

Dwight D. Eisenhower (Republican, 1953–1961)

Stephen Ambrose's comprehensive biography *Eisenhower* (two vols., 1983–1984) remains the best study to date.

John F. Kennedy (Democrat, 1961–1963)

Robert Dallek's *An Unfinished Life: John F. Kennedy, 1917–1963* (2003) is an outstanding and engrossing biography.

Nigel Hamilton's *JFK: Reckless Youth* (1992) is the first of a projected multi-volume study that takes JFK through his first election to Congress.

Jack: The Struggles of John F. Kennedy (1980) and *JFK: The Presidency of John F. Kennedy* (1983), both by Herbert Parmet, were considered the best biographies of Kennedy until publication of the Dallek volume.

Lyndon B. Johnson (Democrat, 1963–1969)

The first three volumes of Robert Caro's yet-to-be-completed biography *The Years of Lyndon Johnson* (1982–2002) are the most detailed life of LBJ. Volume three takes LBJ through his Senate years.

Lone Star Rising: Lyndon Johnson and His Times, 1908–1960 and *Flawed Giant: Lyndon Johnson and His Times, 1961–1973* (1991–98), both by Robert Dallek, are excellent studies of LBJ. Dallek has made great use of the Johnson papers and of numerous oral histories deposited in the LBJ presidential library.

Richard M. Nixon (Republican, 1969-74)

Stephen Ambrose's *Nixon* (three vols., 1987–1991) is a balanced, thorough, and compelling study of Nixon. Volume one, *The Education of a Politician, 1913–62*, is a superb account of these years.

Roger Morris's *Richard Milhous Nixon: The Rise of an American Politician* (1990) is the first of a projected two-volume study.

Gerald R. Ford (Republican, 1974–1977)

There is no good biography available. The best is James Cannon's *Time and Chance: Gerald Ford's Appointment with History* (1993).

Jimmy Carter (Democrat, 1977–1981)

No good biography is available. The best available account of Carter's education is his own book *An Hour before Daylight: Memoirs of a Rural Boyhood* (2001).

Ronald Reagan (Republican, 1981–1989)

William Pemberton's *Exit with Honor: The Life and Presidency of Ronald Reagan* (1998) is the first biography to make extensive use of the material at the Ronald Reagan Presidential Library.

George H. W. Bush (Republican, 1989–1993)

Herbert Parmet's *George Bush: The Life of a Lone Star Yankee* (1997) is a well-written and well-researched study.

Bill Clinton (Democrat, 1993–2001)

No good biography is available, and Clinton's personal papers are still closed to researchers. The best account is the highly selective journalistic account by David Maraniss, *First in His Class: A Biography of Bill Clinton* (1994).

George W. Bush (Republican, 2001–)

The best available book is J. H. Hatfield's *Fortunate Son: George W. Bush and the Making of an American President* (2001).

Internet Resources

http://www.archives.gov/presidential_libraries/index.html
The National Archives and Records Administration holds papers, records, and other historical material related to each of the presidents, and oversees the operation of presidential libraries.

http://memory.loc.gov/
The American Memory collection of the Library of Congress contains a large amount of written, photographic, and audiovisual material useful to understanding American history and the development of education in the United States.

http://www.whitehouse.gov/history/presidents/index.html
This area of the official White House website contains biographies and portraits of each president.

http://www.pbs.org/wgbh/amex/presidents/index.html
This page contains links to brief overviews of each president's life and times, drawn from a public broadcasting series called *The Presidents*.

http://www.americanpresidents.org
This website is based on C-SPAN's *American Presidents: Life Portraits* series. It contains biographical facts and reference materials for each president.

http://www.ipl.org/div/potus/
This database covers the presidents' family lives, schools attended, cabinet members, election results, acts in office, and miscellaneous life events. It also contains many links.

http://showcase.netins.net/web/creative/lincoln/speeches/educate.htm
This web page contains Abraham Lincoln's quotes on the importance of education.

http://www.ux1.eiu.edu/%7Ecfrnb/index.html
The History of American Education Web Project includes short informational articles, biographies of influential educators, and illustrations of educational materials from various periods of American history.

http://www.pbs.org/kcet/publicschool/roots_in_history/index.html
The website "School: The Story of American Public Education" was developed to supplement a PBS series with the same title.

http://www.cedu.niu.edu/blackwell/
The Blackwell History of Education Museum and Research Collections hold many rare and interesting examples of textbooks used in U.S. education over the past two hundred years.

http://www.ed.gov/index.jhtml
The official website of the U.S. Department of Education.

Photo Credits

3: Courtesy of the Mount Vernon Ladies'
Association

4: private collection

7: The University Archives and Record Center,
University of Pennsylvania

8: Manuscript Division, Library of Congress

11: Manuscript Division, Library of Congress

12: Manuscript Division, Library of Congress

13: Manuscript Division, Library of Congress

16: Courtesy of the Harvard University Archives

19: Courtesy of the Harvard University Archives

20: Courtesy of the Harvard University Archives

22: Courtesy of the Harvard University Archives

28: Earl Gregg Swem Library,
The College of William and Mary

31: Earl Gregg Swem Library,
The College of William and Mary

32: Earl Gregg Swem Library,
The College of William and Mary

35: Earl Gregg Swem Library,
The College of William and Mary

37: Earl Gregg Swem Library,
The College of William and Mary

43: Seeley G. Mudd Manuscript Library,
Princeton University

46: Seeley G. Mudd Manuscript Library,
Princeton University

47: Seeley G. Mudd Manuscript Library,
Princeton University

50: Seeley G. Mudd Manuscript Library,
Princeton University

51: Seeley G. Mudd Manuscript Library,
Princeton University

54: Earl Gregg Swem Library, The College of
William and Mary

56: Earl Gregg Swem Library, The College of
William and Mary

59: Earl Gregg Swem Library, The College of
William and Mary

63: Courtesy of the Harvard University Archives

64: Courtesy of the Harvard University Archives

68: Courtesy of the Harvard University Archives

71: Courtesy of the Harvard University Archives

72: Courtesy of the Harvard University Archives

75: Courtesy of the Harvard University Archives

77: private collection

78: private collection

82: private collection

84: private collection

88: private collection

95: Eggleston Library, Hampden-Sydney College

96: The University Archives and Record Center,
University of Pennsylvania

99: The University Archives and Record Center,
University of Pennsylvania

100: The University Archives and Record Center,
University of Pennsylvania

103: The University Archives and Record Center,
University of Pennsylvania

104: private collection

105: The University Archives and Record Center,
University of Pennsylvania

107: Earl Gregg Swem Library,
The College of William and Mary

108: Earl Gregg Swem Library,
The College of William and Mary

111: private collection

117: Wilson Library,
  University of North Carolina, Chapel Hill
118: Wilson Library,
  University of North Carolina, Chapel Hill
121: Wilson Library,
  University of North Carolina, Chapel Hill
123: Wilson Library,
  University of North Carolina, Chapel Hill
127: Old Military and Civil records,
  National Archives and Records
  Administration
130: private collection
131: private collection
137: private collection
138: private collection
142: private collection
144: private collection
147: George J. Mitchell Department of Special
  Collections and Archives,
  Bowdoin College Library
148: George J. Mitchell Department of Special
  Collections and Archives,
  Bowdoin College Library
151: George J. Mitchell Department of Special
  Collections and Archives,
  Bowdoin College Library
152: George J. Mitchell Department of Special
  Collections and Archives,
  Bowdoin College Library
155: Bowdoin College Museum of Art
159: Waidner-Spahr Library, Dickinson College
161: Waidner-Spahr Library, Dickinson College
162: Waidner-Spahr Library, Dickinson College
165: Waidner-Spahr Library, Dickinson College
166: Waidner-Spahr Library, Dickinson College
169: private collection
171: private collection
172: private collection
174–75: private collection
176: private collection
179: private collection
180: private collection
183: private collection
184: Division of Historical Resources, North
  Carolina Department of Cultural Resources
189: private collection
193: West Point Museum Art Collection,
  United States Military Academy

194: West Point Museum Art Collection,
  United States Military Academy
197: Records of the U.S. Military Academy,
  Record Group 404,
  National Archives and Records
  Administration
198: private collection
201: West Point Museum Art Collection,
  United States Military Academy
203: Rutherford B. Hayes Presidential Center
204: Rutherford B. Hayes Presidential Center
207: Rutherford B. Hayes Presidential Center
208: Rutherford B. Hayes Presidential Center
209: Rutherford B. Hayes Presidential Center
210: Rutherford B. Hayes Presidential Center
213: Archives of Hiram College
214: Archives of Hiram College
217: Williams College Archives
218: Williams College Archives
221: Williams College Archives
222: Williams College Archives
225: Archives of Union College
226: New-York Historical Society
229: New-York Historical Society
233: private collection
234: private collection
237: private collection
240: private collection
243: Miami University of Ohio Archives
244: Miami University of Ohio Archives
246: Miami University of Ohio Archives
247: Miami University of Ohio Archives
248: Miami University of Ohio Archives
249: Miami University of Ohio Archives
251: private collection
253: private collection
254: Pelletier Library, Allegheny College
257: Archives of Albany Law School
261: Archives of Albany Law School
262: Theodore Roosevelt Collection,
  Harvard College Library
264: Theodore Roosevelt Collection,
  Harvard College Library
267: Theodore Roosevelt Collection,
  Harvard College Library
268: Theodore Roosevelt Collection,
  Harvard College Library
271: Theodore Roosevelt Collection,
  Harvard College Library

272: Theodore Roosevelt Collection,
  Harvard College Library
275: Manuscripts and Archives,
  Yale University Library
276: private collection
278: Manuscripts and Archives,
  Yale University Library
279: Manuscripts and Archives,
  Yale University Library
280: private collection
282: Manuscripts and Archives,
  Yale University Library
285: Seeley G. Mudd Manuscript Library,
  Princeton University
286: E. H. Little Library, Davidson College
289: private collection
290: Seeley G. Mudd Manuscript Library,
  Princeton University
293: Seeley G. Mudd Manuscript Library,
  Princeton University
294: The Albert and Shirley Small Special
  Collections Library, University of Virginia
296: The Ferdinand Hamburger Archives of
  The Johns Hopkins University
297: Seeley G. Mudd Manuscript Library,
  Princeton University
299: private collection
300: private collection
301: private collection
302: private collection
305: private collection
306: Archives and Library Division,
  Ohio Historical Society
311: private collection
312: private collection
315: private collection
316: private collection
319: Archives and Special Collections,
  Amherst College
322: Archives and Special Collections,
  Amherst College
325: private collection
326: private collection
329: Herbert Hoover Presidential Library
331: private collection
337: Franklin D. Roosevelt Library
339: (top) Franklin D. Roosevelt Library;
  (bottom) private collection
340: Franklin D. Roosevelt Library

341: Franklin D. Roosevelt Library
342: Franklin D. Roosevelt Library
345: Franklin D. Roosevelt Library
347: Franklin D. Roosevelt Library
348: Franklin D. Roosevelt Library
351: Harry S. Truman Presidential Library
  and Museum
352: private collection
355: Harry S. Truman Presidential Library
  and Museum
359: private collection
361: private collection
362: Dwight D. Eisenhower Library
365: Dwight D. Eisenhower Library
366: Dwight D. Eisenhower Library
369: Dwight D. Eisenhower Library
370: Dwight D. Eisenhower Library
372: Dwight D. Eisenhower Library
373: private collection
374–375: private collection
376: John F. Kennedy Library
380: John F. Kennedy Library
381: John F. Kennedy Library
382: John F. Kennedy Library
383: John F. Kennedy Library
385: John F. Kennedy Library
386: John F. Kennedy Library
387: John F. Kennedy Library
389: Lyndon B. Johnson Library and Museum
390: Lyndon B. Johnson Library and Museum
393: Lyndon B. Johnson Library and Museum
395: Lyndon B. Johnson Library and Museum
396: Lyndon B. Johnson Library and Museum
399: Lyndon B. Johnson Library and Museum
401: The Richard Nixon Library and
  Birthplace Foundation
402: The Richard Nixon Library and
  Birthplace Foundation
405: The Richard Nixon Library and
  Birthplace Foundation
406: The Richard Nixon Library and
  Birthplace Foundation
409: private collection
410: Wardman Library, Whittier College
411: The Richard Nixon Library and
  Birthplace Foundation
413: Gerald R. Ford Library and Museum
414: Gerald R. Ford Library and Museum
416: Gerald R. Ford Library and Museum

417: Gerald R. Ford Library and Museum
419: Gerald R. Ford Library and Museum
421: Gerald R. Ford Library and Museum
422: Gerald R. Ford Library and Museum
424: private collection
426: Corbis
429: Jimmy Carter Library and Museum
430: private collection
433: private collection
437: Ronald Reagan Presidential Library
438: Ronald Reagan Presidential Library
441: Ronald Reagan Presidential Library
442: Ronald Reagan Presidential Library
445: Ronald Reagan Presidential Library
446: Ronald Reagan Presidential Library
447: Ronald Reagan Presidential Library
449: Manuscripts and Archives,
    Yale University Library
450: Manuscripts and Archives,
    Yale University Library

451: Manuscripts and Archives,
    Yale University Library
453: Manuscripts and Archives,
    Yale University Library
456: George H. W. Bush Presidential Library
    and Museum
461: private collection
462: (top) private collection; (center, bottom)
    Georgetown University Archives
467: private collection
471: George H. W. Bush Presidential Library
    and Museum
474: Manuscripts and Archives,
    Yale University Library
479: (top right) George H. W. Bush Presidential
    Library and Museum; (left, lower right)
    Manuscripts and Archives,
    Yale University Library
482: George H. W. Bush Presidential Library
    and Museum

Contributors

Editor Fred L. Israel is professor emeritus of American history, City College of New York. He is the author of *Nevada's Key Pittman* and has edited *The War Diary of Breckinridge Long* and *Major Peace Treaties of Modern History, 1648–1975* (five vols.) He holds the Scribe's Award from the American Bar Association for his joint editorship of the *Justices of the United States Supreme Court* (four vols.). For more than twenty-five years Professor Israel has compiled and edited the Gallup Poll into annual reference volumes.

General Editor Arthur M. Schlesinger jr. holds the Albert Schweitzer Chair in the Humanities at the Graduate Center of the City University of New York. He is the author of more than a dozen books, including *The Age of Jackson; The Vital Center; The Age of Roosevelt* (three vols.); *A Thousand Days: John F. Kennedy in the White House; Robert Kennedy and His Times; The Cycles of American History;* and *The Imperial Presidency.* Professor Schlesinger served as Special Assistant to President Kennedy (1961–63). His numerous awards include the Pulitzer Prize for History; the Pulitzer Prize for Biography; two National Book Awards; the Bancroft Prize; and the American Academy of Arts and Letters Gold Medal for History.

Associate Editor Michael Kelly has his doctorate degree in history from the State University of New York, Stony Brook. Dr. Kelly is the author of a forthcoming biography of Senator Robert Wagner. He teaches at the Gilman School.

Associate Editor Hal Marcovitz is a staff writer for *The Morning Call*, Allentown, Pennsylvania. He has written several biographies of presidents for teenagers.

Robert Dallek has taught at Columbia, UCLA, and Oxford. He is professor of history at Boston University. He is the author of a two-volume biography of Lyndon Johnson and *An Unfinished Life*, a biography of John F. Kennedy. Professor Dallek has won the Bancroft Prize, among other awards for scholarship.

J. F. Watts is Dean of the Humanities, City College of New York. He has written extensively on American political and social history.

Bill Thompson majored in history at Boston University. He holds a Master of Divinity degree and is a Presbyterian minister. Mr. Thompson is the author of several books for teenagers.

Daniel E. Harmon is an author and editor. His short story collection *The Chalk Town Train & Other Tales* has received critical acclaim. Mr. Harmon is associate editor of *Sandlapper: The Magazine of South Carolina*.

Anne Marie Sullivan received her baccalaureate degree from Temple University. She is a writer and editor.

Bill Yenne is the author of numerous popular books, including *Astronauts: The First 25 Years of Manned Space Flight*.

Pam Fitzgibbon is a writer. She teaches at the Park School, Baltimore.

Harry Mortimer has two law degrees from Georgetown University. He served as General Counsel, First Fidelity Bank Corp.

Index

numbers in **bold italic** refer to captions